Taken in Time

To Ann, Holly and Daniel

John Briggs
Taken in Time

Photographs of Cardiff's
Docklands Communities at the
turn of the Millennium, 1998-2005

seren

Seren is the book imprint of Poetry Wales Press Ltd
Nolton Street, Bridgend, Wales
www.seren-books.com

© John Briggs, 2005
The right of John Briggs to be identified as the Author of this Work
has been asserted in accordance with the Copyright, Designs and
Patents Act 1988

ISBN 1-85411-364-X
A CIP record for this title is available from the British Library

The publisher works with the financial assistance
of the Welsh Books Council

Front cover:
Pier Head Building and Wales Millennium Centre under construction
Adeola, Oval Basin Entrance
Back cover:
Fisherman, East Dock
Church of St. Mary the Virgin and St. Stephen the Martyr, Bute Street

Printed in Perpetua by Cromwell Press, Wiltshire

Contents

Introduction

This collection of images and accompanying text is the result of photographic explorations since the late 1990s in those Cardiff Docklands communities I first photographed during the 1970s (which led to the publication of my first book, *Before the Deluge*). Given the profound changes taking place in these seminal communities as the new Millennium approached, and driven by my continued interest in them, I felt that an up-to-date photographic response was an urgent and timely undertaking. My new explorations were no less intense, were more detailed in some respects, and led to many new discoveries along the way.

As I began retracing my steps I was inevitably drawn to those sites where the Docklands landscape has altered the most, such as at the old Pier Head, now the Millennium Waterfront with its new bars, shops and restaurants, and around the Inner Harbour, now a freshwater lake following the construction of the Cardiff Barrage. The changes in what is now known as Cardiff Bay have been nothing short of dramatic, the twenty-first-century equivalent of the building of the Bute Docks in the nineteenth, bringing a very different commercial, institutional and human character to Cardiff's largely disused seaport and nearby communities. From that near-derelict, nineteenth-century residential/industrial/maritime environment I had photographed in the mid-Seventies I felt compelled to point my camera at the twenty-first-century service/upmarket housing/leisure-oriented developments that are now preeminent along Cardiff's waterfront.

But some scenarios I encountered were of an unexpected nature. In the midst of all-encompassing new development I found to my surprise that older elements, remains of Cardiff's Victorian and twentieth-century past, still endured. Some historically important, still-working but nearly forgotten institutions, such as the Royal Hamadryad Hospital, the 1840s-era stone warehouses of Edward England Potato Merchants and the pre-World War One workshops of Cardiff Boat Building and Slipway Ltd, amongst others, were still in existence. It was these relics of former Docklands industry and the people still working in them that soon preoccupied me as much as the new institutions that have now replaced them. I didn't want their contribution to Cardiff's stature as a once-mighty industrial and maritime city to go unrecorded as they came to the end of their working days in their Docklands locations. For several of these insitutions this happened while I was photographing them. So *Taken in Time* became part photographic homage to the old (like *Before the Deluge*), in addition to documenting of new entities from which Cardiff is now fashioning its twenty-first-century identity. I consider myself fortunate to have been present at a time of such profound transition in the history of Cardiff's Docklands. However, as will become apparent in this book, I am not an unbiased observer with a camera. It is impossible, having photographed the Docklands over a number of years, not to do so in a way that amounts to a personal response to what has been happening there since the 1980s.

In addition to the radically altered look of the Docklands landscape brought about by major projects such as the Barrage, Mermaid Quay and the Wales Millennium Centre, there is of course the human aspect of Cardiff's Docklands transformation. It is not just the face of the city that has changed, but the faces as well. The number and variety of visitors to Cardiff's reconstructed waterfront is unprecedented. There is as well its modern day workforce in institutions ranging from the political (National Assembly for Wales) to the arts (Wales Millennium Centre). And, of course, one must not overlook the residents of Cardiff's oldest Docklands communities who are still a very prominent part of the city's persona. What Cardiff was and will continue to be depends in large part on the people who are proud to live, or have lived, in the communities of Butetown, Adamsown, Splott and the former Newtown. In some cases I have photographed the same people I encountered in these communities more than 25 years ago. This has been a particularly emotive photographic experience. But now, the even greater ethnic, religious and social mix that has always been a feature of the Docklands communities, from children growing, learning and playing in new environments, to the present generation of immigrants who have arrived from countries in conflict, and on to those who arrive in the Docklands from other towns and cities to work, live or simply enjoy themselves – these, mingling with older inhabitants, contribute to the complex portrait of the Docklands today. Attempting to do justice to this in photographic terms has been a demanding but fascinating business. Aspiring to show the transition from old to new institutions and environments has also been a complex task, but a goal worth aiming for. I would like to think that some justice has been done, for the time being at least. In view of all these elements – what has been put in place, what has been done away with and what has remained at the beginning of the twenty-first century, it has been a truly intriguing time to look at Cardiff's Docklands through a lens.

I have followed basically the same intineraries as I did in *Before the Deluge*. Part One, 'From The Hayes to the Pier Head' starts at The Hayes and follows Bute Street to its end at Mermaid Quay, the former Pier Head. Along the way I have photographed the Butetown/former Tiger Bay community. In Part Two, 'Cardiff Bay and the Docks' I have explored Cardiff's harbour and working docks as redefined by the Barrage and Cardiff Bay. Included are some of the new waterside developments, often a stone's throw from old maritime remains, as well as the still-existent shipping and industrial activity in the working Port of Cardiff. Part Three, 'From Taff to Rhymney: the Edges of Dockland' is devoted to the remainder of older residential communites surrounding the docks bound by the River Taff to the west (The Docks/Rat Island) and the River Rhymney to the east (Adamsdown, Lower Splott and the Rover Way Gypsy Caravan Site). As in *Before the Deluge*, text accompanying the photographs follows in a seperate section at the back of the book.

John Briggs, February 2005

Part One

From The Hayes to the Pier Head
via Bute Street

I wonder how many in present-day Cardiff are aware that there ever was a close association between these two focal points of the city: The Hayes and the Pier Head. It is most likely older Docklands residents who remember the way in which they were linked inextricably, physically and commercially, by a street synonymous with Cardiff's maritime growth, prosperity and decline – Bute Street. At one time Bute Street carried all traffic to and from the Bute Docks towards the centre of Cardiff. It stopped at The Hayes (until 1937 when the section from Bute Terrace to The Hayes was renamed Hayes Bridge Road). Those with business in the docks and Mount Stuart Square, Cardiff's first commercial hub with its offices and banks serving the maritime trade, used Bute Street to get there. Inhabitants of the teeming, multi-ethnic communities of Tiger Bay and the residential Docks used Bute Street when there was need 'to go to town'. Though Cardiff was primarily a coal port, imported produce such as potatoes from Ireland, onions from Brittany, and fish from the seas beyond the Bristol Channel found their way to The Hayes and the city's market via Bute Street. Dockers and sailors of all nationalities used Bute Street's cafés and boarding houses. Pleasure-seekers and ladies of the night used Bute Street's pubs, of which there were many. It was a famous avenue, city-bound towards The Hayes at one end or docks-bound towards the Pier Head at the other. It was documented prominently by Bert Hardy, one of Britain's most renowned photojournalists, in *Picture Post* during the 1950s.

Most of these scenarios are many years distant. Since the mid-1960s, Bute Street skirts Butetown's dreary council estate, once known the world over as Tiger Bay. Rebuilt Tiger Bay's memories are now evoked on pale-coloured pavement squares engraved with the old local names – Cairo Hotel, Waverley, Shirley Bassey, etc. Bute Street's function has become that of community by-way rather than bustling commercial thoroughfare. But if its stature has faded with the fortunes of Cardiff's docks, the Butetown community living along it continues to be a tremendously varied and lively one. Lifelong residents are proud of their past and extremely concerned about their future as changes around and within the estate make an impact on their lives. If not so much Bute Street itself, then certainly its community needed to be photographed for the new Millennium.

More dramatic in recent times is what has happened at either end of this once world-famous, mile-long stretch of tarmac. Major redevelopment has transformed both its extremes, in the centre of the city and at the waterfront, since the 1980s. The Hayes in the city centre is probably busier than ever. It is on the way to the St. Davids Centre and Queen's Arcade shopping malls. Commuters arrive by the busload or by car using the nearby multi-storey car parks, concert-goers enjoy the adjacent St. David's Hall, café-goers flock to the nearby café-quarter of Mill Lane, and legions of sports fans cross it on their way to the Millennium Stadium or Wales Ice Rink. It is an ever-busy crossroads where some will stop for a snack or cup of tea at the time-honoured and spruced-up Hayes Island Snack Bar/Bwty Hayes. None of the above-mentioned leisure/shopping/sports facilities existed when I photographed The Hayes in the 1970s, although it was the city's inner hub even then. Time to take a camera there again.

At the docks end of Bute Street, once known as the Pier Head, I don't think the changes could have been imagined by the average Cardiffian even ten years ago. Where Bute Street meets the water's edge, Mermaid Quay now prevails. Not a quay in the traditional seafaring sense but a collection of voguish bars, cafés and restaurants. There is nightclub entertainment, a bank, estate agents and designer shops. It has an attractive landing stage from which water buses depart for the Barrage, Penarth or a trip up the Taff to view the Millennium Stadium. Clowns and street artists entertain on the waterfront promenade, which is dotted with sculptures to remind those who know, or to instruct those who don't, of Cardiff's maritime heritage. However, standing at the Pier Head today, it's impossible to conjure up an image of Cardiff in the days of constant and visible maritime activity: ships coming from the world over to load Welsh coal, paddle steamers boarding passengers for day-trips to Weston, dredgers keeping the harbour channels open, vessels putting in for repairs at the drydocks, etc. Gone also is the museum that once imparted a sense of the past. What used to be the Inner Harbour with the second highest tides in the world is now the freshwater lake of Cardiff Bay. As in the city centre, old docklands scenarios have been replaced by the prodigiously consumer-oriented projects of twenty-first-century Cardiff. Significant new ground for the photographer to cover. So once again I tread the path I did in the 1970s, starting at The Hayes and, after a small diversion or two, head down Bute Street.

Breton 'Shoni', Onion Seller, The Hayes

Family of Football Fans

Railroad Bill

Newsboy outside David Morgan's Department Store

Shoppers at The Hayes Bus Stop

Architectural Detail, Caroline Street

Tony's Fish and Chip Bar

Colin's Books

Chris Anthony, Hairdresser

Mrs B. Tucker, formerly of Mill Lane Market

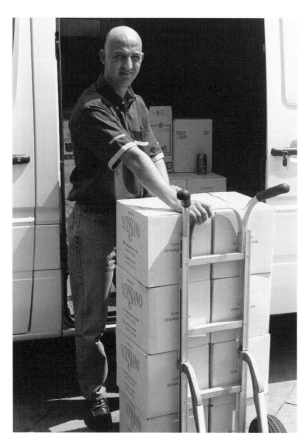

Deliveryman, Mill Lane

Young Man outside 'The King's Cross'

Mill Lane Café Quarter

Sam's Bar

'All Hands' Sculpture, Custom House Street

Muslim Girls in front of 'All Hands' sculpture

Window Repairs, 'The Golden Cross'

Statue of Jim Driscoll, Bute Terrace

Multi-storey Car Park, Tredegar Street

In front of the former New College

'Docks' Sign near Bute Street

Pedestrians, the Bay Express and Bute Street Railway Bridge

Muslim Lady and Football Fans, Bute Street

Exterior of 'The Crown'

Behind the Bar

Two Pub Regulars

Two Friends in 'The Crown'

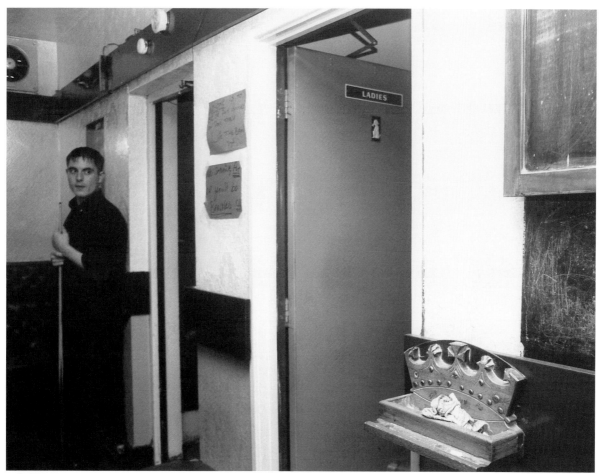

Pub Games

'The Crown' Chalk Tray

Stables, John Street

Bill Kennedy, former Resident of John Street

Bill Kennedy and Fred Hissey

Traveller, Bute Street/John Street

Skateboarders, Callaghan Square

Statue of John Crichton Stuart

Figures in the Rain, former East Wharf

Ty Gobaith/Hope House, Bute Street

Railway Bridge over the former Junction Canal

Rahman

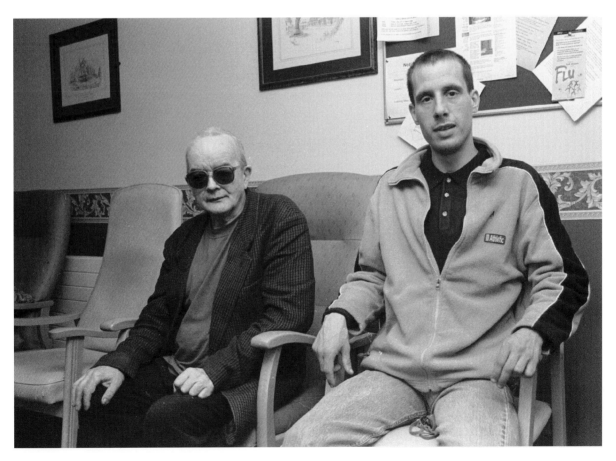

Gareth and Mark

Angelina Street before Renovation

New Houses under Construction, Angelina Street

Church of St. Mary the Virgin and St. Stephen the Martyr, Bute Street

United Harmony Singers in Concert

Humie Webbe and United Harmony Singers in Rehearsal

United Harmony Singers

Sheik Said and Worshippers, Alice Street Mosque and Islamic Centre

Men at Prayer

The Mosque Dome and Minaret

Hannah Street Congregational Chapel and Mosque Minaret

Orthodox Congregation at the Great Easter Service

Dome of St. Nicholas, Greek Orthodox Church

Nicoletta, Greek Student

Church Committee Members

Elderly Worshipper and Icon

Mahmoud Kahlinleh, ex-Merchant Seaman

Traditional Dress in Bute Street

'Clivey' and Olive

Ladies in Loudoun Square

Young Man outside Loudoun Square Shops.

Two Butetown Elders

Fatima Ingram, South Loudoun Square

Mrs Emmanuel, Butetown Pharmacy Assistant, and Customer

Ghulam Hussain and Nasir Ahmad, Grocers/Newsagents, Loudoun Square

Mohammed Adan, Rose of Sanna Somali Café

Dean Mohammed, Butcher, Loudoun Square

Abdul Rahman,
Loudoun Square Fish Shop

Roy Stanley Jenkins,
Butetown/Tiger Bay resident

Fatimah Girgrah, Butetown Community Centre

Lady Bingo Player

Neil Sinclair and Dunstan Ross, Bute Street

Brian Ahmed and his Son, Marshalla

Audrey Scott and Kathleen Blades, in front of Maria Court Mosque

Butetown Playgroup, Canal Park

Pupils from Mount Stuart Primary School

Young Girl Mountaineer

Marcia Blades and her Son, Isaac

Joseph, St Cuthbert's School Pupil, Immtech Studios

Patti Flynn with Victor Parker Photo, Butetown History and Arts Centre

Seafarers Group with Mr Bill Wright (seated, second left)

Façades in Mount Stuart Square

The Cory Building

Former Butetown Post Office and Midland Bank

Ship Lane

Café Bar, Mermaid Quay and Cardiff Bay

Part Two

Cardiff Bay and the Docks

Redevelopment in Cardiff's Docklands has taken place on a truly massive scale, given that huge tracts of land around the disused Bute Docks and on the former East Moors Steelworks site became available in the 1980s for ambitious new ventures. Back then, the blueprint for a grand design that would transform the whole of south Cardiff was drawn up by the Cardiff Bay Development Corporation. As a result there are now many pristine, twenty-first-century engineering, commercial, residential, cultural and leisure projects to photograph — Mermaid Quay, the Oval Basin Project, St. David's Hotel, the Barrage and the Wales Millennium Centre, to name the most prominent. And there is much yet to come. This book will have been published before the opening of the Debating Chamber of the National Assembly for Wales in 2005 and before the completion of the International Sports Village. In their turn these will command great attention in Cardiff Bay.

But also harking back to the past of the original Bute Docks, I was able to photograph some historically important remains even though many traces have been eliminated. The site of the West Dock, filled in by the time I first trod over it in the 1970s, may be covered by new apartments, but it still retained one or two older buildings awaiting conversion: the Edward England warehouses in particular attracted my attention. The Victorian-era Granary, which once stood at the edge of the West Dock, was also earmarked for redevelopment, but was alas demolished in late 2004. Nearby, new infrastructure 're-uniting the city with its waterfront' as the developers and city fathers would have it (Bute Street no longer fulfills this function, apparently), has replaced the old Collingdon Road. The supposed gap is now bridged by Lloyd George Avenue, a four-lane boulevard that runs the length of Bute's first dock. My first objects of maritime fascination in this area in the 1970s, the Norwegian Church and the Junction Dry Dock with its Victorian buildings, are long gone. Thankfully the church was rebuilt in 1989, relocated at the water's edge where the Roath Basin lock meets Cardiff Bay. At the docks end of Lloyd George Avenue, the Oval Basin, once the antechamber for the West Dock next to the Pier Head Building, has been re-excavated to a certain depth and the resultant large open space, covered in wooden decking, hosts high-profile waterfront events.

Turning my photographic attention to the East Dock I found that it has been retained, albeit in truncated form, as a water feature for public enjoyment and private development along its former wharves. Fishermen and joggers use its historic quaysides. The Roath Basin, separated from the East Dock but still integrated into the docks system, is now a popular visitor area, especially when naval vessels or sailing craft tie up along Britannia Quay on its north side. The *Goleulong* lightship is permanently moored there as a Church in Wales visitors' centre. However, commercial shipping activity in Roath Basin ceased in 2003 when the last sand wharf was cleared; adjacent to it the water-filled Bute Dry Dock lies forever dormant. It was here that I discovered one of the very last maritime businesses before it moved in 2003 — Cardiff Boat Builders. It was a unique experience to be able to photograph a company that had started in 1913 making wooden lifeboats. The two docks which remain active, the Roath and Queen Alexandra, are where shipping is now concentrated in the modern-day port. Here too, I was able to photograph the remains of past maritime industry, such as the landmark

Spillers grain silo, before it was swept away. I then focussed on newer facilities that have been put in place as Cardiff docks diversify in order to become profitable once again. Scrap metal, oil, sand, container shipping, steel and timber have long taken over from the coal upon which Cardiff's success was built. Former drydocks, the Mount Stuart and the Commercial, exist now to provide a fashionable maritime environment for the expensive apartments, offices and leisure facilities built around them. The others, the Bute and the Channel, await whatever posterity has in store even if they still held, until recently, reminders of their former days as mainstays of Cardiff's ship repairing industry.

Of course the Barrage and its effect upon Cardiff's former harbour could not help but command my photographic attention. The permanent high water level in what is now called Cardiff Bay has so completely transformed the maritime environment that only a photograph taken at low tide, such as in *Before the Deluge*, could give the uninitiated an idea of what the harbour was like in pre-barrage days. The ancient wooden 'dolphins' and the century-old paddlesteamer landings remain, but permanently up to their waists in water. These are still presided over, thankfully, by the Pier Head Building, Cardiff's former symbol of seafaring prosperity. In turn, its pre-eminence is now challenged by dominant new edifices standing nearby, in particular the Millennium Centre. But at the opposite end of Cardiff Bay it is the Barrage that has decided the city's destiny and that now symbolises the transformation that has taken place as Cardiff turns away for good from its industrial and seafaring past towards a service- and leisure-oriented future.

Cardiff Barrage, View from Penarth

Cardiff Barrage Visitors

Norwegian Church and new Cardiff Bay Buildings

'Dolphin' and Mermaid Quay

Pier Head Building, and Wales Millennium Centre under Construction

Pier Head Building Detail

Leon Charles, Tiger Bay Poet/Rapper

Kyle Legall, Tiger Bay Artist

Oval Basin Fountain and Wales Millennium Centre

Adeola, Oval Basin Entrance

End of Bute Street, Mermaid Quay

Mobile-phone User

Staff of 'The Spice Merchant' Restaurant

Visitors to Mermaid Quay

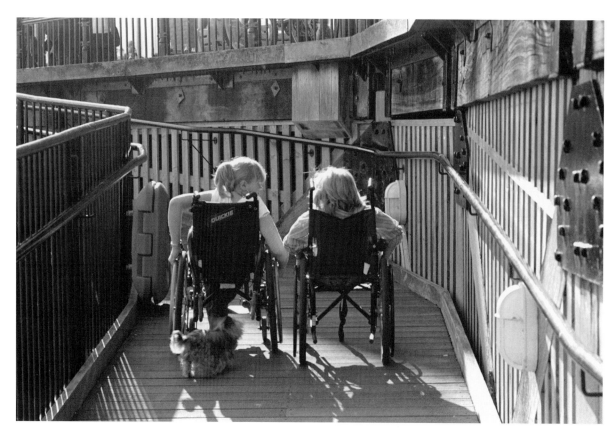

Disabled Visitor Access at Mermaid Quay

Keith Monroe, Cardiff Barrage Road Train Driver

Barrage Train, Stuart Street

Academi Staff in the Wales Millennium Centre

Sharon, Reception Desk, Red Dragon FM Studios

Owen Leslie, ex-Merchant Seaman, East Dock

'The Wharf', East Dock

1920s-era Electric Crane

Former Bailey's Offices, Bute Dry Dock

Lock Gate, Roath Basin

Craftsmen, Cardiff Boat Builders

Ken and Peter, Cardiff Boat Builders' Tea-room

Office, Pictures of Small Craft

Launch of the *Pembrey*, Cardiff Bay

71

Port Banner, Roath Basin

Dredger *City of Cardiff*

Bows of *Goleulong 2000* Lightship

Lightship Tower and Masts of Sailing Vessel *Prince William*

Entrance to Roath Dock

Stern of *Hallgarth* Tugboat

Eversmeer Loading at Dowlais Wharf

Docks Diesel Shunter

Demolition of Spillers Mill, Roath Dock, 2002

Spillers Mill, 2003

1905 Pontoon, Roath Dock

Channel Dry Dock Entrance and St David's Hotel, Cardiff Bay

Barge, Channel Dry Dock

Cardiff Bay Buildings, from Channel Dry Dock

Anchors, Lloyds Beal, Dumballs Road

Quayside, Steel Coils and 'A' Sheds

Oil Tanks, Queen Alexandra Dock

RMS *St. Helena*

Lock Supervisor Seeing off *Welsh Piper*

Lock Supervisor Peter Davis and Lock Gateman John Davis

Part Three

From Taff to Rhymney:
the Edges of Dockland

From its centre to the sea, it's easy to think of Cardiff's transformation as taking place along a north-south axis. But to picture the full scope of Cardiff's redevelopment one must also explore it from the Taff at the Docklands' western edge to the Rhymney in the east. So starting in the Docks community nearest the Taff, known as Rat Island, I followed a path along James Street to the new Lloyd George Avenue and then to former Newtown, on to Adamsdown, Splott and finally to the Rover Way gypsy community before reaching the eastern foreshore and the still-tidal Rhymney.

The terraced streets of Rat Island remain basically intact. It is just north of them on the industrial strip of land between the river and Dumballs Road once occupied by Curran's mighty factories that upmarket riverside apartments have been built. These I photographed during an excursion up the Taff. The Royal Hamadryad, the former Seamen's Hospital, is Rat Island's most memorable structure. I was able to photograph both inside and outside the ornate late-Victorian facility just before it closed in mid-2002. Such a monument to Cardiff's past must not be consigned to oblivion.

Moving eastward along James Street it was difficult to visualize the area as I photographed it in the 1970s with its terraced streets, shops and pubs soon to be bulldozed for the construction of the Louisa Place estate. Some familiar places and faces remain, such as those one sees in 'The White Hart', but solicitors offices and one or two shops catering for a mix of office workers and locals show how much things have changed from the days when James Street served mainly dockers, seafarers and Docks people.

As James Street skirts the edge of Mount Stuart Square it is easy to catch a glimpse of Cardiff's nineteenth-century grandeur. Heading straight towards Bute Street, however, the massive contours of the Wales Millennium Centre loom large: it is obvious that one is about to enter another dimension. The neo-classical colonnade of the disused Post Office stands as a last bastion of the Docks' past before the new monoliths of the twenty-first century – the Wales Millennium Centre, Atlantic Wharf Leisure Village – take over.

At this point I turn into Lloyd George Avenue, where the land once bordered the Bute West Dock. On more than one occasion my eye has been attracted by long lines of coaches and stretch limousines unloading football fans along this new boulevard. Heading for the Millennium Stadium, they walk past the old relics, anchors and grabs, street ornaments from the past, before noticing the photographer snapping pictures of them. I couldn't help but wonder at the changes responsible for bringing about this scenario as I then focussed on the tower of the Pier Head Building in the distance.

The Edward England potato warehouse at the northern extremity of Lloyd George Avenue was the scene of an impromptu tour in 2002. The owner saw that a photographer friend and I were taking an interest in the building and offered to show us around, allowing us to take photographs not long before the warehouses received their last consignment of potatoes and closed their doors after 160 years. Conversion into flats is almost complete at the time of writing.

Nearby Tyndall Street has seen many changes. It once ran past Newtown, 'Little Ireland' as it was known, before its terraced streets were demolished in the 1960s. The vacant site was being used by gypsy caravans when I photographed there in the 1970s. Today, Tyndall Street Industrial Estate is home to a number of small business units. Two young ladies from the Nature's Table health food company obliged for the camera as I spotted them on their break. Nearby, office girls and shoppers climbed the steps of the old footbridge that was once the link between the Irish of Newtown and the city centre.

At the end of Tyndall Street, on a small parcel of land obscured by overgrown shrubbery and left over from the days when countless railway wagons passed through Tyndall Street Crossing on their way to the docks and steelworks, I witnessed the end of the line for three long-standing businesses at their Docklands location: East Dock/Mossi's Café, Pogson & Sons Engineering, and Machinery Movements Crane Hire. Nowhere in the Docklands have I seen the transition from past to present take place more abruptly as they vanished within days of each other in mid-2003. The café finished for good, the other two relocated – the last survivors of their kind in the docks. Within a few months a new automotive dealership was established.

Moving east to retrace my 1970s steps through Adamsdown, I found certain landmarks enduring – the Black Bridge and Adamsdown Gospel Hall. People stay put as well. The next generation of the Camilleri family (who appeared on the cover of *Before the Deluge*) live in the same Constellation Street house as their parents. 25-strong this time, three generations plus friends posed at the back of the house on a fine day in 2001. In Splott, however, Loretta and Dorothy Chambers could only stand at the gates of Moorland Park, a few yards from where their original family home had stood. On a happier note, some of Splott's older residents from Selwyn Morris Court's sheltered housing complex were photographed enjoying a night out at 'The New Fleurs', an iconic neighbourhood club that survived the almost total demolition of lower Splott in the 1970s. Ken Norton, heavyweight boxing legend, was captured on film during his visit to the Fleurs thanks to the now-retired owner Dai Furnish's connections in the boxing world.

I mentioned previously the gypsy caravans that for a time occupied the ground where Newtown's houses had stood before the mid-1960s. The gypsies themselves moved sometime around 1980 when a purpose-built council site was provided in Rover Way at Splott's eastern edge. Photographing residents young and old here showed me that in the last 25 years their close-knit community has perhaps been less subject to the forces of change than other communities. The pattern of their existence over time is, to me, not unlike the regular rise and fall of the tide that continues undisturbed along the foreshore just beyond the boundary walls of their designated territory.

I felt that it was fitting to finish with a photograph of Cardiff's eastern shore at low tide. In one way, it is a reminder of the scene which used to be an everyday occurrence in Cardiff's harbour, in another it is a sign that even in these days of great change, some things do remain constant.

Swans in the Taff, Clarence Bridge

Rear of Bute Esplanade, the Docks

Royal Hamadryad (former Seamen's) Hospital, Rat Island

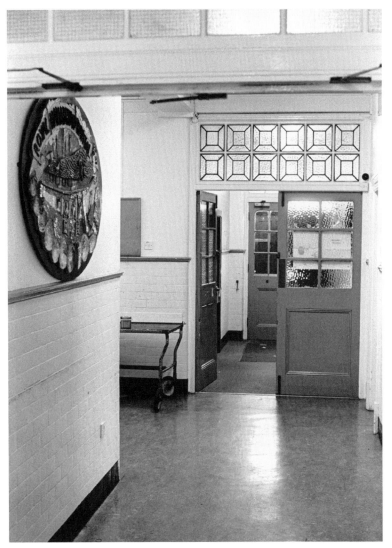

Entrance Hall

Kitchen Staff on the Last Day

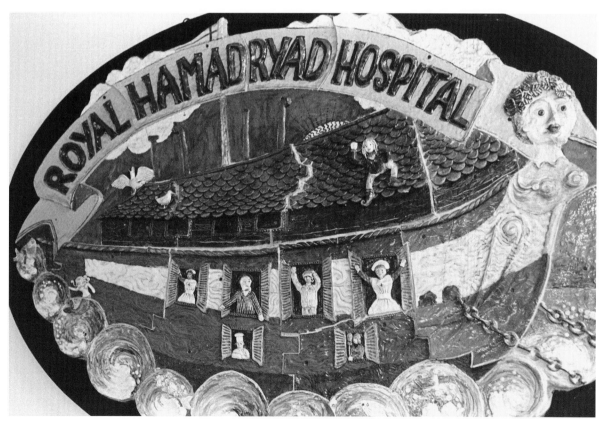

HMS *Hamadryad* Plaque

Salvage House, Clarence Road

Ronnie Keith and Harry Cooke, James Street

Drayman outside 'The White Hart'

Sixth Formers at 'The Ship and Pilot'

Former Canal Warehouses near James Street

Tourist Bus and former Pumping Station

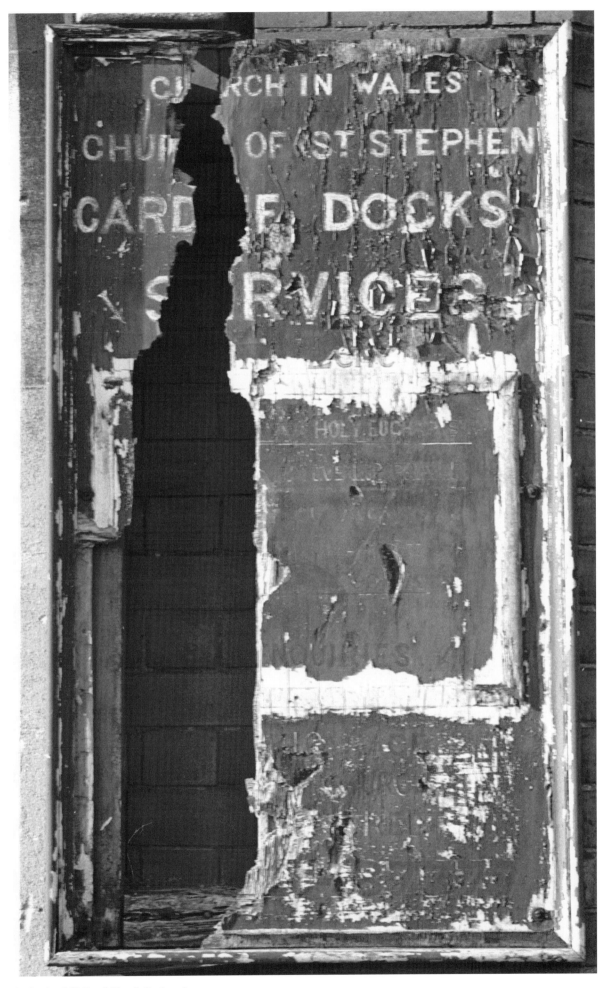

St. Stephen's Hall and Church Signboard

Post Office Pillars, Bute Place

Rear of Louisa Place Estate

Post Office detail

Railings in Bute Crescent

Cycle Route Signpost, Lloyd George Avenue

Cardiff Bay (former Bute Road) Station Canopy, New Apartments

Pier Head Building, National Assembly Debating Chamber Site

New construction in Lloyd George Avenue

Football Coaches, Lloyd George Avenue

Redundant Road Signs, Butetown

Father and Son, English Football Fans

Passage between Lloyd George Avenue and Bute Street

Sacks of Potatoes, Edward England Warehouse Interior

Edward England Potato Warehouse, Exterior

Interior detail

Herbert Street and Tyndall Street, former Newtown

Employees, Tyndall Street Industrial Estate.

Ladies on steps of the Newtown Footbridge

Demolition Team and Passing Ladies, Herbert Street

Demolished Timber Merchant's Offices, Herbert Street

Power Station, East Tyndall Street Bridge

Demolition Worker

Jaki and Rosemary, East Dock/Mossi's Café

Rosemary and Marina

Breakfast at East Dock Café

Harry, Tugboat Crewman

Talking About Mossi's

Last Day, Empty Tables

Dale, Motor Engineer, Pogson's Engineering

Lou Pogson

Piston-boring Machine

Hand Tools, Pogson's Workshop

Pogson's Demolished Works, East Dock/Mossi's Café

Derek and Louise Davies, Machinery Movements Crane Hire

Crane Driver

Crane Yard Worker

John Sennett, Adamsdown Historian, 'The Great Eastern' Pub

Young Mum and Friend on the Black Bridge, Adamsdown

Young Muslim on the Black Bridge

Gospel Hall, Kames Place

Yvonne Camilleri, Adamsdown Resident

Camilleri Family and Friends in Garesfield Street

Adamsdown Children, Anderson Field

Detail in South Luton Place, Adamsdown

Sikh Gentleman in South Luton Place

Loan Shop, Constellation Street

Moira Hotel, Moira Terrace

Loretta and Dorothy Chambers, Splott

Chambers Sisters, Pointing at their Initials

Graham Kingston of Aberystwith Street

Playing in Aberystwith Street

Ken Norton, Boxer, at 'The New Fleurs', Splott

Rita, formerly of Newtown

Beryl and her Tattoos, 'The New Fleurs' Club

Statue and Caravan, Rover Way Gypsy Site

Daily Cleaning, Rover Way

Tom Price and two Grandsons

Tom Price and his Gypsy Stallion

Baby Agnes and her Granddad

Trisha Smith and Children

Trisha Smith

Agnes Coffey with her Daughter, Helen

Small Craft on the River Rhymney

Foreshore near Rover Way

Acknowledgements

I am indebted to all those allowed themselves to be photographed for *Taken in Time* in their communities, their homes, their places of work, leisure and worship. I am particularly grateful to those who made further photographs and the recording of factual detail possible, as well as to those who promoted my work once my collection of photographs was complete. Without the support of the following, this book would not have been possible.

Karen Allen; Norwegian Church Arts Centre

Kathleen Blades; Butetown

Yvonne, Tony and Janine Camilleri; Adamsdown

Dorothy and Loretta Chambers; Tremorfa, formerly of Splott

Leon Charles; Barry, formerly of Butetown/Tiger Bay

Harry Cooke; Docks

Frank Courie; Butetown Pharmacy, Loudoun Square

Rosemary and Modestino Cucciniello; Canton, formerly of East Dock Café

Derek and Louise Davies; Machinery Movements Crane Hire

Adeola and Scott Dewis; Grangetown

Davina Driscoll; Cardiff City Council Children's Play Services

David Furnish; formerly of 'The New Fleurs', Splott

Fatimah Girgrah; Butetown Community Centre

Fred, Mark and Dorothy Hissey; Grangetown

Hugh Irwin; Ty Gobaith Salvation Army Centre

Dennis Jenkins; Butetown

Mahmoud and Doreen (i.m.) Kahlinleh; Butetown

Bill Kennedy; Butetown

Ann Moloney; Adamsdown, formerly of 'The Crown'

Phil Williams; Pogson's Engineering

Tom Price; Rover Way Gypsy Site

Abdul Rahman; Loudoun Square Fish Bar

Sharon Randall-Smith; Mount Stuart Primary School

Gwenda Richards; HTV Wales

Sheik Said; Alice Street Mosque and Islamic Centre

Seafarers Group; Butetown History and Arts Centre

John Sennett; Adamsdown

Lyn Shell; Cardiff Boat Builders and Slipway Ltd.

Neil Sinclair; Butetown/Tiger Bay

Julie Smith; Associated British Ports

Trisha Smith; Rover Way Gypsy Site

Humie Webbe; United Harmony Singers, Butetown

Karen and Carole Wicks; Splott, CCHA Selwyn Morris Court

Part One: From The Hayes to the Pier Head via Bute Street

9   Breton 'Shoni', Onion Seller, The Hayes

Onion sellers have been coming to Cardiff since the nineteenth century and continue to do so in the twenty-first, either selling their produce from The Hayes or on foot from door to door in various Cardiff neighbourhoods. The sellers themselves are now in their twenties, carrying on from the 'Shoni onions' of old and often from the same families or villages as the older generation. However, as in the case of this young Breton 'shoni', selling onions in Cardiff was a means of improving his English and financing his studies back in France rather than providing the long-term livelihood that it had for his predecessors.

10   Family of Football Fans at The Hayes Island Snackbar/Bwty Hayes

With the number of large-scale sporting events, especially football and rugby, having dramatically increased in Cardiff since the completion of the Millennium Stadium, The Hayes Snack Bar is a popular refreshment stop for many stadium-bound visitors not just from Wales but from all parts of Britain. This family has come from Lincoln to watch their team in the divisional play-offs.

Railroad Bill

Those who walk through the shady confines of The Hayes, especially at the weekend, whether shopping or arriving for a big international match, will inevitably be entertained by buskers and street acts. The Hayes is still one of the city's most popular spots for street entertainment. This is Railroad Bill, a skiffle band from Cardiff, performing hilariously as only they know how.

11   Newsboy outside David Morgan's Department Store

A seemingly permanent fixture of The Hayes, which I first photographed in the 1960s, is the newsbox outside David Morgan's department store. The newsboys who man it are undoubtedly a breed apart, masters of the Cardiff quip, resolute vendors of the *Westen Mail* and *Echo* in all weathers and able to tell at 20 paces whether you've got the right change for a newspaper. David Morgan's closed in January 2005.

Shoppers at The Hayes Bus Stop

A change of road layout and extension of the pedestrianised area around The Hayes has also made it one of the busiest bus stops in the city. More people now converge on this urban half-acre than perhaps ever before. In contrast to the past, when the area was at the town end of Bute Street and saw porters carting fresh produce or sailors on leave walking up from the docks, it is now city-centre-bound shoppers from all parts of Cardiff who disembark at The Hayes in search of consumer delights.

12   Caroline Street Architectural Detail

Few must be those who visit Caroline Street, one of the oldest byways in Cardiff, to gaze at its architectural features, but they are worth more than a passing glance. They tell of style, craftsmanship and attention to detail from a bygone era, for decades now relentlessly disappearing from Cardiff's Victorian streets.

Tony's Fish and Chip Bar, Caroline Street

One of the oldest, and with Dorothy's right next door, one of the best-known chippies in the city. Social class notwithstanding, Tony's and Dorothy's are culinary bywords in Cardiff. Known colloquially as 'Chip Alley', Caroline Street is home to no less than ten door-to-door chip/kebab shops, cafés and small restaurants along a stretch of road little longer than a rugby pitch. And on the days of rugby internationals when the nearby Millennium Stadium is filled to its 72,000 capacity, there is undoubtedly a chip cone made ready for every fan in anticipation of the many thousands who will visit Caroline Street before or after the match. But how much longer Caroline Street's oldest establishments will last into the new century is a matter for conjecture. Cappuccino and chips?

13   Colin's Books, Caroline Street

Food for thought, though not of the purest kind, is still available for consumption in Caroline Street. Plastic barrier sections are a sign of the forthcoming pedestrianisation with piazza-style paving, presumably more worthy of the new upmarket establishment of the Brewery Quarter, across the street from Colin's.

Chris Anthony, Hairdresser, Caroline Street

A respected member of Cardiff's Greek Cypriot community and Caroline Street's last resident of the older generation, Mr Anthony set up his barber shop in 1943, above which he still lives. Custom is rare but old friends stop in to have a chat. Harking back to the days when the local man-about town went to have his haircut at Chris', his shop is an icon of the many small businesses that once thrived in the streets around The Hayes.

14   Mrs B. Tucker, formerly of Mill Lane Market at her Produce/Flower Stall

Just around the corner at The Hayes end of Caroline Street is Mill Lane, where Cardiff's open-air market was a prominent city feature from the 1940s to the 1970s. Produce stalls are now to be found in St. David's Market, a modern but pale reincarnation of Mill Lane market, hidden away behind the St. David's Shopping Centre. A survivor from Mill Lane, Mrs Tucker is perhaps the longest serving open-air stallholder in Cardiff and she continues to operate her St. David's Market stall daily after 40 years in the fruit and vegetable trade.

Deliveryman, Mill Lane

Thirty years ago, when I first photographed in Mill Lane, the market-workers pushed hand trucks loaded with boxes of lettuce and cauliflower to and from its produce stalls. Nowadays, the handcarts are used to shift boxes of mineral water, crates of wine and alcopops from white delivery vans to Mill Lane's outdoor cafés and bars.

Young Man outside 'The Kings Cross', Mill Lane

'The Kings Cross' is a familiar Mill Lane fixture and for decades has been a meeting place for Cardiff's gay community, some dressing up for the occasion in attention-getting attire.

15   Mill Lane Café Quarter

Mill Lane has undergone several reincarnations in the course of its history. In the nineteenth century and part of the twentieth it ran along a stretch of the Glamorganshire Canal as it passed through the city. In the twentieth century from the 1940s to the 1970s it was lined with the produce stalls of the city's busiest outdoor market. In the twenty-first century it is now established as Cardiff's café quarter where parasols, wavy metal barriers, awnings and other café paraphernalia lend the street something of a continental air. It has fostered a new breed, the Cardiff café goer, unknown before the 1990s, who now enjoy a whole street dedicated to eating and drinking à la terrasse.

Sam's Bar, Rugby Fans

Thanks to the popularity of the café quarter in recent years, Sam's at the St. Mary Street end of Mill Lane has attracted a more cosmopolitan crowd compared to its former black-leather-jacketed, heavy-metal-loving clientele. These Welsh rugby aficionados hail all the way from Porthcawl and are in town to see Wales play at the Millennium Stadium.

16 'All Hands' Sculpture, Custom House Street

This work by sculptor Brian Fell, unveiled in 2001, stands in homage to the Glamorganshire Canal and the bargees who pulled their narrow boats along it using ropes in places where horses couldn't go, such as through the canal tunnel under the city streets. It is located next to 'The Custom House' (1845) which once overlooked the former East Wharf of the Glamorganshire Canal. East Wharf and West Wharf are no more, having disappeared in 2001 beneath the new tarmac extension of St. Mary Street. Behind the sculpture stands what is left of the former Central Hotel, a Cardiff landmark damaged by a disastrous fire in early 2003.

Muslim Girls in front of 'All Hands' sculpture

Two younger generation Cardiffians, perhaps from the nearby Butetown community, make a striking contrast to the massive steel fists behind them, symbol of Cardiff's industrial/maritime past.

17 Window Repairs, 'The Golden Cross', Custom House Street

To repair a window in most Brains houses these days would require replacing a large pane of plate glass. Since the 1980s the brewery has systematically removed the traditional leaded glass windows, bearing the Brains name in a blue and white diamond-shaped panel such as the one in the photograph. These were a renowned Cardiff architectural feature, as well known as the stained glass windows of any Cardiff church. Now they are gone in all but a few Brains pubs in an attempt, it seems, to shed their old-fashioned image. 'The Golden Cross' windows, one of the few sets that have been allowed to survive and a vital feature of Cardiff's most splendid example of Victorian pub architecture, here receive the attention of the repair man.

18 Statue of Jim Driscoll, world-champion Cardiff boxer, Bute Terrace

Standing watch over the city's transformation 'Peerless Jim' Driscoll, the famous Cardiff boxer, has been fixed in time at a corner where only one of Cardiff's older buildings remains that he would have known in his day "The Golden Cross'. What would he make of Bute Terrace were he alive today? Given the chance, he would no doubt be boxing in the Wales National Ice Rink across the street.

Multi-storey Car Park, Tredegar Street

In the 1980s, quaint and narrow streets off Bute Terrace such as Mary Ann and Tredegar were unceremoniously transformed into access routes for multi-storey car parks. Gone was the mix of small shops and commercial vitality typical of this part of the city, superseded by these concrete monsters. This is the usual Saturday morning scene in Tredegar Street, in fact the only activity seen here any day of the week

19 In front of the former New College, Bute Terrace

Months before the structure is completed, the passers-by already seem minuscule in comparison to the new apartments under construction behind the 1896 façade of the former Victorian building. But the human scale will be even more insignificant compared to the domineering height of the new tower. Does this mean that there is a vision for a Cardiff skyline akin to that of American cities?

'Docks' Sign near Bute Street

This obsolete-looking sign in Bute Terrace is no longer of any use to docks-bound traffic. Instead, the fortuitous blending of its message with the 'For Sale' banner behind it neatly sums up the process going on in the Docklands since the 1980s. Present-day institutions, such as the insurance company that occupied the office building behind the 'For Sale' banner, make it obvious that service industries, rather than maritime business, are now the mainstays of Cardiff's livelihood.

20 Pedestrians, the Bay Express and Bute Street Railway Bridge

The bridge under which the people and the bus have just emerged was traditionally the dividing line between town and the Docklands. The avenue is Bute Street, Cardiff's most famous and formerly notorious street. It still does carry a lot of pedestrian traffic, in spite of there no longer being any pubs, cafés, shops and small businesses along the way for people to stop at. These days it is simply a conduit for shoppers and their cars going to and from the city centre, sports fans going to and from their coaches and the Millennium Stadium, Butetown residents going to and from the city centre less than a mile from their homes, and people with their jobs in new Docklands businesses going to and from work.

Muslim Lady and Football Fans, Bute Street

An interesting yet not untypical moment of human encounter in Bute Street where people of different cultures cross each other's paths as much as ever. In this instance, a Butetown resident in traditional dress shares the street with football fans from faraway Bournemouth sporting their own ritual garb and heading for the Millennium Stadium.

21 Exterior of 'The Crown', facing Bute Street

A momentary step back in time. After all the old Bute Street pubs nearest town such as 'The Custom House' and 'The Glastonbury Arms' had gone, 'The Crown' hung on for a few more years, playing host to an intriguing mix of people. It was razed in 1998 and the site where it stood on the corner of John Street and Bute Street at present remains car parking space.

Behind the Bar of 'The Crown'

The décor of the pub was very much 1970s, with smooth mahogany planks lining the walls and partitioning the drinking areas. Mock Chesterfield seats provided the seating. Old handpumps are still in evidence, though in the pub's final days, they were decorative rather than functional. On a weekday morning the barmaid had plenty of time to sit for the photographer.

22 Two Pub Regulars

Having something quirky in common with the same finger is obviously cause for mirth for Norman the pub minder and friend. The handwritten sign on the wall was also a feature of 'The Crown' and obviously an attempt by its last landlady Anne Moloney to get her clientele to observe certain rules of pub etiquette.

Two Friends in 'The Crown'

'The Crown' was one of very few pubs in Cardiff at the time (1998) where their closeness was accepted and not considered unusual.

23 Pub Games in 'The Crown'

The pool table at the back of the pub was well-patronised,

this player typical of those energetic young men who were its regular users. By this time pool had years since replaced 'arrows' as the usual pub competition, but as late as this 1997 scene, the chalkboard shows there is a dartboard still in use. The landlady's handwritten sign proclaims 'No smoking pot or you'll be banned'. Drugs had apparently started to become a problem.

'The Crown' Chalk Tray

The jewel in the pub's crown, or rather the crown itself, was this hand-carved wooden chalk tray, engraved with the year 1977, the year of the Queen's Silver Jubilee. Wholly fitting that the pub named after the monarch's headgear should commemorate the occasion in this way and have a unique replica for use by its dart-playing regulars.

24 Stables, John Street

John Street is an L-shaped cul-de-sac, named after the Second Marquis of Bute, John Crichton Stuart. Joining Bute Street at one end but then taking a perpendicular bend at the other it continues a short distance before finishing at the railway viaduct leading to Cardiff Central station. It is along this part of the street that some of Cardiff's oldest buildings survive, having come under the ownership of the Welsh National Opera in the 1990s. Known as The Stables, they are a row of small cottages with a wide courtyard entrance. It is here that WNO props are made and stored. Before the WNO these buildings were the premises of J.W. Wisbey & Co. Ltd, a joinery specialising in shop fitting and shop front building.

Bill Kennedy, former Resident of John Street

During the 1990s the Welsh National Opera built their new headquarters on the site of the old John Street Court, Lane and houses. Bill stands on the spot where the house in which he was born, No 6, once stood.

25 Bill Kennedy and Fred Hissey

Bill (left) insists that this tiny area was an island on its own, not a part of Tiger Bay/Butetown which began on the other side of Bute Street, and not a part of Newtown, just the other side of the railway embankment behind Wisbey's yard. He and his brother-in-law Fred stand against the stone cottages on the east side of John Street, these being similar to the ones on the west side in which Bill was born and lived for over 30 years until they were demolished in 1958. Conditions were 'a bit primitive', Bill recounted. The water tap was behind the front door, there was no drainage so after washing you threw the water out in the street. Communal toilets as well as coal-fired washing boilers were in John Street Court behind the row of houses numbered 3-10. The houses were designed to accommodate two families, one in the front room the other in the back, and sleeping was done upstairs in four small bedrooms – a 'four-up, two-down' arrangement. The coal bunker was under the stairway between the two downstairs rooms and clouds of black dust descended upon the family if the coal merchant happened, as he sometimes did, to make his delivery whilst they were at table. The candle stand Bill is holding was used to find his way in the dark, electricity-free house (there was one gaslight at the end of the street) and Fred is holding a horseshoe which he saved from the door to the communal toilets in John Street Court. Fred was born behind Scriven's the butchers, near the corner of John Street and Bute Street. Part of his working life was spent at sea, where a maritime accident left him short of two fingers, temporarily put back on his hand by a photo-retouch artist for his wedding photograph. He then worked for years in the Channel Drydock whereas Fred

was in the Royal Navy before joining the docks labour force as a rigger, working there until he retired.

26 Traveller, John Street/Bute Street

Probably oblivious to the history and former appearance of this once lively corner, the traveller, perhaps on his way to Central Station, could symbolize the brusque and determined fashion in which this part of Cardiff has been completely transformed since the late 1990s. His gaze is directed at the new office building in Callaghan Square where the well-known 'Custom House' once stood.

Skateboarders in Callaghan Square

It was first named Bute Square but then changed to Callaghan Square in honour of Cardiff's most famous political son who was British Prime Minister in the 1980s. Nonetheless it is the statue of John Crichton Stuart, Second Marquis of Bute who presides over Cardiff's newest central public space. His twenty-first-century minions are mainly skateboarders who congregate in their dozens on the weekend.

27 Statue of John Crichton Stuart, Second Marquis of Bute

Twenty-first-century lighting fixtures have been juxtaposed with the Victorian statue of the 2nd Marquis of Bute as he surveys Callaghan Square and faces towards the city centre. He stood for many years at the top of St. Mary Street, facing the docks, before being moved to his present location in 2002. In the background are the new apartments built on the former site of the Bute West Dock, the first in Cardiff, which the Marquis opened in 1839.

Figures in the Rain, former East Wharf

Without the shelter of the railway bridge which once spanned East and West Wharf these employees from the new Callaghan Square office building on their left are clearly feeling the effects of a Cardiff shower. They are no doubt unaware that the Square occupies the site of old Crichton Street, formerly a red light area and historically the location of the Greek Cypriot community. In the distance are the tower blocks in what was once Tiger Bay, the first of Cardiff's docklands communities to be redeveloped in the 1960s.

28 Ty Gobaith/Hope House Salvation Army Centre, Bute Street

A now-familiar Bute Street landmark, Ty Gobaith was opened in 1976 to replace the old Salvation Army hostel, a former Victorian commercial building. Its greatly-enlarged capacity provides temporary accommodation for 61 men and the professional staff there give residents training, advice and support aimed at getting them to live independently in the community.

Railway Bridge over the former Junction Canal, Bute Street

The bridge is one of Cardiff's few remaining nineteenth-century structures along Bute Street and stands directly opposite Ty Gobaith. Whereas the Junction Canal used to run under it, now a newly-installed path links Bute Street with Lloyd George Avenue on its other side. Years ago, the old canalside path under the bridge was used to gain access to Collingdon Road and West Bute Dock from Bute Street. It was also used in the 1950s film *Tiger Bay*.

29 Rahman

With Britain in general and Cardiff in particular becoming an ever more cosmopolitan society, it is not surprising that organizations such as the Salvation Army provide their services to a more ethnically diverse clientele.

Gareth and Mark

Sitting in one of the day rooms are two residents of different generations. Gareth, the older, has benefitted for many years from the shelter and care provided by the Salvation Army and knew the wooden 'bunk-in-a-dormitory' style accommodation in the old Bute Street hostel. He now lives independently. Mark, the younger of the two, is waiting for a placement in the near future.

30 Angelina Street before Restoration

One of the Butetown council estate's two remaining pubs in the late 1990s, 'The Bosun' was razed to make way for the construction of Red Sea House, a residence for elderly Somali seamen. The 'problem' maisonettes behind it were soon to follow. The view is of Angelina Street looking towards Butetown/Tiger Bay's 1960s-era tower blocks, Nelson Nouse and Loudoun House.

New Houses under Construction, Angelina Street

The maisonettes built in the 1960s had fallen into a state of disrepair and become such a haven for criminal activity and vandalism that Cardiff City Council had them demolished before starting to build new housing units in the summer of 2003. This is probably the first instance of major regeneration Butetown has seen since the clearance of Tiger Bay's terraced streets and the building of the Butetown council estate, the tower blocks of which are again seen in the background. Local tenants began taking occupancy of the new properties in early 2004.

31 Church of St. Mary the Virgin and St. Stephen the Martyr, Bute Street

Butetown's oldest surviving landmark and religious building is St. Mary's, serving the religious needs of the local Anglican community since 1843. Facing Bute Street and just a short distance from Ty Gobaith its towers can be seen from anywhere in Butetown and many other vantage points in the city. This modern-day perspective is from behind Butetown railway embankment where trees and daffodils grow along the new Lloyd George Avenue

United Harmony Singers, in Concert

One of Butetown's most popular and talented groups, the United Harmony Singers entertain a full church audience with a mixture of modern, jazz and gospel favourites. Under the direction of Humie Webbe, they are just as at home performing in St. David's Concert Hall as in St. Mary's Church. The group sings in support of charity, local organisations and at major cultural events in the city.

32 Humie Webbe and the United Harmony Singers in rehearsal

Practising a gospel number at their weekly rehearsal in the old Butetown 'slipper baths'. Hands moving and bodies swaying are vital to the performance.

United Harmony Singers

The members of the choir rehearse weekly and are local either to Butetown or to other nearby communities.

33 Sheik Said and Worshippers, Alice Street Mosque and Islamic Centre, Butetown

Sheik Said, in the centre of the group and Imam of the Mosque since its opening in 1980, has been for decades a highly respected leader of Cardiff's Muslim community. He came to Cardiff in 1939 at the age of 9 after his father, a Yemeni seaman, was killed at sea in one of the first ships to be torpedoed at the start of World War II. After completing his religious training in the Yemen, Sheik Said became Imam of the Nur Ul Mosque in Peel Street,

Wales' first, in 1956. He was there until its demolition in the mid-1970s, and when the Alice Street Mosque was completed in 1980, he was chosen as its leader.

Men at Prayer, Alice Street Mosque

Shoes are removed and ablutions performed as acts of purification before entering the main prayer space of the mosque. Standing, bowing and prostration are all outward signs of prayer and these are led by the Imam, the appointed minister of religion, who speaks first in Arabic, then in English and finally in the national language of the majority of the worshippers.

34 The Mosque Dome and Minaret

The fine copper dome and slender minaret of the mosque complement each other in eastern Arabic style, constituting another of Butetown's religious landmarks. The tower is a symbol of the call to prayer which takes place five times a day. The mosque was completed in 1980 to serve Butetown's growing Muslim population and is one of two in the community.

Hannah Street Congregational Chapel and Mosque Tower

Less than a hundred yards from the mosque stands the minuscule Hannah Street Chapel, a perfect example of the closeness to each other of places of worship in Butetown. Sadly, the tiny Hannah Street Chapel, which traces its roots back to 1867 and which has served its congregation in this small building for over 40 years is now empty and facing an uncertain future at the time of writing. It was officially closed in 2003 after the death of the last member of its congregation.

35 Orthodox Congregation at the Great Easter Service

In a dramatically visible sign of communal celebration, the Christian Orthodox worshippers take flowers off the epitaph, a symbolic representation of Christ's tomb, at the end of the Great Easter service.

Dome of St. Nicholas Orthodox Church

It is impossible not to marvel at the number and architectural variety of churches which have served different faiths in the Butetown community since the nineteenth century. The Greek Orthodox Church of St. Nicholas in Greek Church Street has, since 1906, served the Greek and Christian Orthodox community once centered in nearby streets but now spread throughout Cardiff and south Wales. At one time there was an important Greek and Greek Cypriot community near the Church, the consequence of Greek seafaring men coming to Cardiff when it was one of the busiest ports in the world.

36 Nicoletta, Greek Student

Not a Greek resident of Cardiff but a visitor to St. Nicholas, Nicoletta has just finished attending the Great Easter service. She holds the flowers she has removed from the epitaph.

37 Church Committee Members

Older gentlemen sit on heavy carved wooden chairs at the entrance to the nave, the central area for worship. In front of them is a basket in which members of the congregation place money for lighted tapers or candles that they will devoutly place in front of saints' icons in the narthex, or church vestibule.

Elderly Worshipper and Icon

Dressed from head to toe in austere black, signifying that she is a widow, the elderly lady worshipper attends the Orthodox Great Easter Mass at St. Nicholas. She comes from the right side of the nave, where female worshippers sit whilst the men sit on the left.

38 Mahmoud Kahlinleh, Somali ex-Merchant Seaman

Mr Kahlinleh is Butetown's most senior Somali resident, having come to Cardiff in 1937. From running a lodging house for Somali seamen in Angelina Street he went to sea during the Second World War and survived being torpedoed three times. As a result of his distinguished service, he was decorated with the Atlantic Star, the Africa Star, the Italy Star and the George Silver Medal. After the War, Mr Kahlinleh married his Newport-born bride Doreen and became one of the leaders of the Somali community in Butetown. His fund-raising efforts were vital to the building of the Maria Court Mosque.

39 Traditional Dress in Bute Street

Patterns and colours are sometimes strikingly flamboyant, determined by the country and region of the wearer rather than by religious affiliation. This style of dress is frequently seen in what continues to be Wales' most cosmopolitan avenue

'Clivey' and Olive

Ivor Paris ('Clivey'), whose mum is from St. Kitts, and his partner Olive Powell, whose dad is Spanish and mum Welsh, were both born and raised in Butetown. They are pictured here outside the house they share in Bute Street. Olive works locally in the Butetown Pharmacy.

40 Ladies in Loudoun Square

Sandra Herbert (left), who lives in 'the Bay' (as Butetown is still referred to by its residents) is in the company of her friend Henrietta Long. Both ladies are in conversation with former resident Leon Charles and he is asking them what they think of the Butetown community today. This immediately raises an indignant and impassioned commentary on the lack of amenities, poor shopping facilities and poor housing in contrast to the multi-million pound private developments now surrounding the former docks-dependent community, statistically the most deprived ward in Cardiff.

Young Man outside Loudoun Square shops

Eugene Toby's father is Algerian and his mother from Cardiff. He is a frequent visitor to 'the shops' where he can meet up with his peers. For young men of his age (20 years old) with little money and no employment there isn't really anywhere else to go.

41 Two Butetown Elders

Mr Gerald Ernest, on the left, and his Somali friend bring the bleak environment of the Loudoun Square Shops to life with some lighthearted banter and a shared smile for the camera. A number of the shop units have been disused for years, presenting a depressing outward appearance, but this does not seem to affect the spirit and cheerfulness of older residents. Gerald's father was from St. Lucia and mother from Barbados, but ask him what his nationalty is and the answer comes out in one word: 'Welsh'. And like most who still have vivid memories of Tiger Bay and the Docks, Gerald Ernest cares deeply about the community in which he has lived for 80 years. He regularly mans the reception desk at the Butetown History and Arts Centre and started his volunteer work in the 1980s when the organization's first home was in St. Paul's Methodist Church, Loudoun Square.

Fatima Ingram, South Loudoun Square

A warm, sunny day in Loudoun Square, the same as could be said of Fatima Ingram's smile. The house which she shares with her husband is on the south side of Loudoun Square where, in the mid-nineteenth century fine Victorian townhouses were built for those getting rich from Cardiff's booming docks and coal export trade. When the wealthy forsook Loudoun Square for the newer city suburbs, immigrants and newcomers from all parts of the globe began to settle there, eventually making it one of the most racially mixed areas in Britain. Fatima's ancestral family, like so many others, came to Butetown in those circumstances.

42 Mrs Emmanuel, Butetown Pharmacy Assistant, and Customer

Mrs Emmanuel, of Tanzanian origin, has worked at the pharmacy for over fifteen years, treating clients of all nationalities with professionalism and dignity.

Ghulam Hussain and Nasir Ahmad, Grocers and Newsagents, Loudoun Square

Ghulam Hussain (left) and Nasir Ahmad (right), both originally from Pakistan, have been serving their clientele at the local shop for some 23 years. In addition to having conversations with their customers in English they will just as frequently do so in Urdu and Punjabi.

43 Mohammed Adan, Rose of Sanna Somali Café, Loudoun Square

Open for breakfast, the café has no sign and is very sparsely furnished – plastic chairs, a couple of tables pushed together, no till, no sign of any menu, orders are simply given to the owner at the kitchen door. Nonetheless, Mr Adan is a busy man serving the many Somali men for whom the small café is an important gathering place.

Dean Mohammed, Butcher, Loudoun Square

Butetown's only butcher is Dean Mohammed, who as a boy in the 1970s started working in his father's shop in Maria Street. When the old Butetown shops were razed in the mid-1960s the business moved to its present premises, a purpose-built unit in Loudoun Square which Dean eventually took over from his father. It is particularly important that he provides Halal meat for his Muslim customers.

44 Abdul Rahman, Loudoun Square Fish Shop

Of Pakistani origin and known to locals as 'Ray', Mr Rahman has lived in Cardiff since 1961 and been proprietor of the local 'chippie' for 28 years. His first job was as a maintenance worker on British Rail wagons and his second was as a Cardiff bus driver. Here he happily displays his Butetown Community Award. The awards are made annually as a way of giving recognition to those who work particularly hard at promoting good relations within the community and who serve as an example to others.

Roy Stanley Jenkins, Butetown/Tiger Bay Resident

Born in Jamaica in 1919 and raised there, Roy served with the U.S. Army in the Panama Canal Zone during World War II. After his honourable discharge in 1948, he came to the UK with his British passport, staying briefly in London then moving to Cardiff and finding accommodation in the Docks. Rationing was still in effect and he remembers living poorly at first, though eventually he was able to buy a house next to 'The Freemason's Arms'. He became a singer in a big band and an impresario, travelling all over the UK. As he moved about with his band, Roy collected money with the charity box shown in the photograph. Amongst other causes he asserts that the money he helped to raise contributed towards the filling-in of the old

Glamorganshire Canal which once ran through Butetown. This he termed a 'death trap' for children when it fell into disuse in the 1960s and became a water-filled but very dangerous playground.

45 Fatimah Girgrah, Butetown Community Centre
Butetown Community Centre has existed for over 60 years, though the present building dates from the redevelopment of Tiger Bay in the 1960s. Fatimah is in charge of the Pensioners' Association and sees to it that one of the Centre's most popular activities, the Tuesday bingo session, runs without a hitch. Although the 25 or more ladies who attend are from many different ethnic backgrounds, they are united in their singing of the Welsh National Anthem 'Hen Wlad fy Nhadau', at the start of each bingo session.

Lady Bingo Player, Butetown Community Centre
Concentration so intense, the photographer is worried his presence and the camera shutter's click are a nuisance.

46 Neil Sinclair and Dunstan Ross, Bute Street
Author and community spokesman Neil Sinclair, born in Frances Street, holder of an MA from the University of California and still living locally in Loudoun House, continues to concern himself with community affairs. Neil's two volumes, *The Tiger Bay Story* and *Endangered Tiger* are his detailed, first-hand accounts of life in Tiger Bay with insights into the significance of this unique community for Cardiff and south Wales as a whole. He has worked indefatigably at removing the stigma and prejudiced views that have dogged the area throughout its history. Walking along Bute Street Neil will invariably stop every few yards to have a chat, in this case with Dunstan Ross, of Barbadian extraction, long-time friend and former Butetown resident.

Brian Ahmed and his son, Marshalla
Brian is a long-time resident of Bute Street whose father was Somali and mother Welsh. Born in Stuart Street, he is keen to point out that he is a 'Docks' and not a 'Bay' boy. His son Marshalla is also proud of his multi-racial roots.

47 Audrey Scott, Kathleen Blades in front of Maria Court Mosque
First photographed by me in 1975 in front of the old Peel Street Mosque, Audrey and Kathleen stand in the same place in front of the rebuilt Mosque. Both are now mums with children of their own and still live locally.

48 Butetown Playgroup, Canal Park
When I photographed children in the area during the 1970s, the street was their playground more often than the council estate's open green space, once the site of the Glamorganshire Canal. That large space, these days known as Canal Park, now sees up-to-date playground and fitness equipment as well as excellent play schemes run by Cardiff City Council Children's Services during the school summer holidays. This group of young but fearless mountaineers is preparing to go up a ten-metre portable rock face to develop their climbing skills. Left to right: Pierre, Hasheem, Mica, Anisah, Niomi and Ibrahim.

Pupils from Mount Stuart Primary School
From the largest of the three Butetown junior schools, the other two being St. Cuthbert's and St. Mary the Virgin, this class shows in no uncertain terms that the diversity typical of the Butetown community since the nineteenth century is just as apparent among its younger generation today as it was in the past. Their spirit of co-operation made it easy, from a photographer's point of view, to take an appealing group portrait. I couldn't help but think that the children's positive attitudes augur well for the future of good human relations in their community.

49 Young Girl Mountaineer
Not just a winning smile; she couldn't get enough of going up and down the rock face, each time more quickly than the last.

50 Marcia Blades and her Son, Isaac
Marcia, sister of Kathleen in an earlier photograph (p47), is from a large Butetown family of West Indian origin, of which Isaac is the newest member.

Joseph, St. Cuthbert's School Pupil, Immtech Studios
Primary school pupils from the three Butetown junior schools are learning how to use radio broadcasting equipment as part of their technology syllabus. Immtech Studios, a Butetown media and music technology training centre set up in a unit of the former Curran factory in Dumballs Road, provides them with the necessary tuition and state-of-the-art facilities. As part of their training, each pupil does a two-minute radio broadcast in the role of DJ for a local pop-music radio station.

51 Patti Flynn with Victor Parker Photo, Butetown History and Arts Centre
The Cardiff jazz guitarist and singer, Vic 'Narker' Parker is a Tiger Bay legend. Butetown's modern-day diva Patti Flynn, Tiger Bay (Maria Street) born and bred, credits him with being her mentor. She is also an author, creator of the text for *Fractured Horizons*, a work combining her writings with photographs of Cardiff's seascape outside the Barrage.

Seafarers Group with Mr Bill Wright, Butetown History and Arts Centre
The Seafarers Group at the Butetown History and Arts Centre meets regularly to keep the seafaring and industrial history of the docks alive. Former owner of Cardiff Boatbuilders and Slipway Co. Ltd, Mr Bill Wright, poses here with regular members of the Seafarers Group whom he addressed in May 2003. He talked about the history of the docks-based institution, founded by his father in 1913 and eventually taken over by himself, responsible amongst other things for the design and construction of wooden lifeboats for the Merchant Navy and passenger ships.

52 Façades in Mount Stuart Square
With most of its architecture fortunately still intact since Victorian times, a visit to Mount Stuart Square will give the observer an idea of what Cardiff's commercial hub looked like when it served the world's busiest coal port a century ago. Although it was originally a residential area for the well-to-do, it eventually became home to the banks, shipping companies and colliery export offices connected with Cardiff's booming maritime trade. Rows of distinctive façades and porticoes facing the square exemplify the neo-classical style of the era.

The Cory Building
The Cory Building was at one time the offices and headquarters of one of Cardiff's greatest shipping families. Today it plays host to a number of disparate modern-day organizations. With one or two exceptions, the long-gone coal export trade echoes as a distant memory in Mount Stuart Square. Yet due to some timely commercial investment, the area has, for the most part, physically and commercially managed to survive the ravages of time and change.

53   Former Butetown Post Office and Midland Bank
Two more attractive Victorian buildings, surviving examples of those institutions formerly the cornerstones of Cardiff's business and financial sector, remain at the intersection of Bute Street, Bute Place and James Street, once the busiest corner of the Docks. The Midland Bank is still operational while the Post Office in the foreground, originally built as the Mercantile Marine Office in 1874, has stood empty for many years awaiting whatever fate developers have in store for it.

54   Ship Lane
Except for the graffiti, basically unchanged since I first photographed it in 1975, Ship Lane runs behind a row of surviving older buildings on the west side of Bute Street.

Café Bar, Mermaid Quay and Cardiff Bay
At the end of Bute Street and from an elevated vantage point in the Mermaid Quay complex, this view shows the permanent high water level in Cardiff Bay with the Barrage and Penarth Head in the distance. The café bar letters in the foreground give a significant hint at the kinds of establishments that now proliferate along the capital's trendy waterside bar, restaurant and shopping precinct.

Part Two: Cardiff Bay and the Docks

57   Cardiff Barrage, View from Penarth
Taken from the headland of Penarth this view shows the Cardiff Barrage, opened in 2000. It measures 1.1 kilometres in length, cost £220 million and when being built was Europe's largest engineering project. The Barrage has transformed Cardiff's spectacular mudflats and hugely tidal Inner Harbour into a permanent freshwater lake, now known as Cardiff Bay, fed by the rivers Taff and Ely at its northwest end. Across the bay are the structures of the city's new waterfront schemes including the St. David's Hotel (centre) and Mermaid Quay (right). Anticipated economic benefit came at a price: the disappearance of an internationally important wildlife site (an SSSI); the risk of damage to local housing due to raised groundwater levels; and huge budget overspend.

Cardiff Barrage, Visitors
Two couples, one from Wales the other from France, enjoy fine weather on a visit to Cardiff's newest maritime showpiece. The large canvas sails behind them, intended to remind visitors of a yacht in full sail, overlook an observation deck and picnic area.

**58   Norwegian Church and
new Cardiff Bay Buildings**
More of the new is in evidence as the camera pans further along the eastern shoreline of Cardiff Bay. To the left of the rebuilt and relocated Norwegian Church are the NCM Credit Insurance Building and National Assembly for Wales.

'Dolphin' and Mermaid Quay
A nineteenth-century structure retained as a water feature for visitors to the Millennium Waterfront, this is one of five which once stood above a gridiron platform. Probably last used in the 1950s, small ships would tie up to these moorings for cleaning and minor maintenance, settling onto the gridiron at low tide. This, and several other dolphins stand side by side in Cardiff Bay as in the days when the Inner Harbour was devoted to the comings

and goings of coal-filled vessels mingling with the pleasure steamers that tied up on the opposite side of the harbour. In the background is Mermaid Quay, the retail and gastronomic centrepiece of Cardiff's redesigned waterfront.

**59   Pier Head Building and Wales Millennium
Centre under construction**
The Pier Head Building once overlooked the Inner Harbour, a landmark for approaching ships as they passed to the left or right into the Bute Docks. Now it overlooks the pleasure boats and other craft small enough to pass through the Barrage. Behind it the Wales Millennium Centre, which opened in late 2004, begins to take shape.

Pier Head Building Detail
'Dwr a Than' – Water and Steam. These were the elements that made possible the Industrial Revolution and brought about Cardiff's success as the world's greatest coal port 100 years ago. The key phrase in Welsh is embedded in the terracotta tilework of the Pier Head Building, dating from 1896 when the docks were working at full capacity and receiving more vessels than they could efficiently handle.

60   Leon Charles, Tiger Bay Poet/Rapper
A vociferous critic of money spent on Cardiff Bay and the Barrage compared to the lack of investment, poor facilities and dearth of prospects for the young in his native Butetown, Leon recites some of his verse at the Oval Basin near the Pier Head Building. As a distinctive local voice he is regularly invited to work with young people in schools and community organizations both in Cardiff and the Valleys.

Kyle Legall, Tiger Bay Artist
Of the many talented individuals the Docklands communities has produced, Kyle is probably the hippest due to the number of large murals he has been commissioned to paint whether it be in Butetown/Tiger Bay's Canal Park, the Butetown Youth Pavilion or on the front of yet-to-be-occupied units in Mermaid Quay. His paintings are invariably inspired by places and people from Tiger Bay and the Docks. Kyle also designs his own clothes and footwear.

**61   Boy at Oval Basin Fountain
and Wales Millennium Centre**
Until the 1960s, this area was part of the ship's basin leading to the Bute West Dock. Restored in the 1990s and renamed the Oval Basin, the space is now overlooked by a tall, chrome-plated fountain shimmering as ripples of water cascade down its sides. It also stands in front of the gargantuan new home for the performing arts, the Wales Millennium Centre. The crowd seen here is gathering for its official opening in November, 2004. Nonetheless it is the fountain rather than the Centre's imposing inscriptions that inspires awe in the young man.

Adeola, Oval Basin entrance
Adeola Dewis is an artist from Trinidad now living in Cardiff who, apart from applying herself intensely to her own work, is much involved in modern dance and works at the Millennium Centre as a tour guide and arts workshop tutor. I wanted her to do something powerfully and attractively human that would contrast with the usual weekday spectacle at the Oval Basin, that of people walking like small insects across a large expanse of floor, dominated by the massive outline of the Wales Millennium Centre. The resulting leap was a satisfyingly vivid gesture.

62   End of Bute Street, Mermaid Quay
Bute Street meets twenty-first-century commerce: Mermaid Quay's bunting festoons its shopping mall, restaurants and bars.

Mobile-phone User
Mermaid Quay's facilities are tailor-made for the mobile-phone generation. The contemporary environment would not be complete without them.

63   Staff of 'The Spice Merchant' Restaurant
The exotically-themed 'Spice Merchant' offers diners in Cardiff Bay the best of Indian cuisine. Half a century ago the same building was famed for its European cuisine as confirmed by the plaque between the pillars honouring the French chef Albert Magneron. It was then known as 'The Windsor Hotel', or 'The Big Windsor' by locals, and so it remained until it fell on hard times during the 1990s and closed down. For several years there was a question as to whether this famous Docks landmark would survive until it was bought by two brothers, Sheikh and Mikealim Alhada. These already successful Bangladeshi restaurateurs, willing to invest enough money to restore the Windsor to something like its former glory, assured its rebirth as 'The Spice Merchant' after renovation work costing £1.8 million. Pictured are some of the 33 full and part-time Bangladeshi staff at the restaurant, which opened in early 2003.

64   Visitors to Mermaid Quay
Fine weather brings many hundreds of visitors, especially at the weekend and during the summer holidays. The ramp in the foreground gives access to the quayside at water level where people may board excursion boats for a a crossing to the Barrage, a trip around Cardiff Bay, or up the River Taff to view the Millennium Stadium. The stairway in the background leads to the restaurants on the upper level of Mermaid Quay where diners can enjoy a number of different types of cuisine as well as views across the Bay.

Disabled Visitor Access at Mermaid Quay
The design of Mermaid Quay's ramps and walkways helps ensure full access for wheelchair-bound visitors, giving them the opportunity to enjoy one of south Wales' newest and most extensive leisure-oriented development.

65   Keith Monroe,
Cardiff Barrage Road Train Driver
Keith, a native Cardiffian from Splott, is the driver of the Barrage Train which departs every hour from Mermaid Quay. An alternative for those who don't fancy using the waterbuses to cross Cardiff Bay, Keith's train uses a route that goes through the active Port of Cardiff to get to the Barrage. His homespun commentary along the way is as enjoyable as the journey itself, as he evokes the days of Cardiff as the greatest coal port in the world and points out various locations, such as the old dock gates, where there are no visible traces of the past. His commentary with regard to present day institutions such as the National Assembly for Wales is also astute, declaring that giving free bus travel to OAPs is easily the best thing Welsh AMs have done. The return journey is to the melodious strains of a Welsh male voice choir intoning 'Myfanwy'. At the Barrage Keith's train stops for fifteen minutes to either drop off passengers who wish to stay and catch a later train back to Mermaid Quay, or to give them a quarter of an hour to enjoy Cardiff's greatest innovation since the building of the Bute Docks. A more genial host and font of local knowledge you could not hope to encounter.

Barrage Train, Stuart Street
The train's one and only pickup point is in Stuart Street in front of the new public car-park. Local people will remember that this was the junction of Stuart Street with Louisa Street, one of several terraced streets in the old Docks community.

66   Academi Staff in the Wales Millennium Centre
In addition to being Cardiff's definitive venue for the performing arts and home to the Welsh National Opera, the Wales Millennium Centre also accommodates other important arts-based institutions. One of these is Academi, the Welsh literature promotion agency. These youthful members of Academi's staff, typical of the present-day workforce in Cardiff Bay and seen here organizing their new office, make an interesting historical contrast to the burly dockers and seafaring men who once held sway in this area, formerly near the old dock gates.

Sharon, Reception Desk,
Red Dragon FM Studios
Cardiff's Bay's entertainments complex, Atlantic Wharf Leisure Village, covers part of the former West Dock site. Red Dragon FM occupies pristine purpose-built studios in the new edifice and stands approximately where the original Norwegian Church used to. From its modest beginnings in a near-derelict part of the city, Red Dragon now enjoys great success as Cardiff's local radio station with its youth-oriented pop-style format. With an instinctively cheery smile, Sharon at the reception desk ensures that visitors always get a good first impression at Red Dragon FM.

67   Owen Leslie, ex-Merchant Seaman, East Dock
Mr Leslie, better known as 'Les', an ex-merchant seaman from Belize who settled in Cardiff, was first photographed by me in the well-known 'Custom House' pub in Bute Street in 1977. The pub has since been demolished, but Les continues to live in Tyndall Street, not far from the East Dock. This is territory familiar to him from his seafaring days where he poses for the camera once again in 2003.

68   'The Wharf'
'The Wharf' attracts mainly young pleasure-seekers to the East Dock who eat, imbibe and enjoy live entertainment in a mock-Victorian setting. In contrast to the multitude of modern but often bland styles in Cardiff Bay, here is a welcome echo of the nineteenth-century buildings once typical of Cardiff's dockland. Located where Hills' Dry Dock and Engineering used to repair ships, it makes use of the entrances to the former dry dock bays as part of its outdoor drinking area.

1920s-era Electric Crane
Another token reminder of Cardiff's past, this 1920s era vintage crane stands on its own on the East Dock quayside. A common sight at one time, it may well have worked across the dock at Hills' Dry Dock and Engineering.

69   Former Bailey's Offices, Bute Dry Dock
A now-forlorn docks landmark, Bailey's former offices is the last complete industrial structure still standing in the Roath Basin area apart from a tiny, derelict locks cottage. The flooded Bute Dry Dock in the foreground is where ships had been repaired since the nineteenth century and where the first steam-powered vessel in Wales was launched. The dry dock was most recently used as the site for the construction and floating of concrete sections for the Barrage.

Lock Gate, Roath Basin

At the entrance to Roath Basin and motionless for years now. Once they moved day and night to allow for the movement of ships between the basin, the docks and the Inner Harbour.

**70 Craftsmen, Cardiff Boat Builders
and Slipway Ltd.**

This trio of skilled personnel are employed by one of the oldest Cardiff docks-based businesses to survive into the twenty-first century. They face the camera just before the launch of the high-powered cruiser *Pembrey*, the last craft to be restored in the Cardiff Boat Builders workshop before demolition in May 2003. The workshop stood next to Bailey's offices at the side of the Bute Dry dock.

Ken and Peter, Cardiff Boat Builders' Tea-room

Ken, in his 70s, is the company's oldest employee and remembers well the days when the bread-and-butter activity of the works was the making of wooden lifeboats for passenger ships and Merchant Navy vessels. Since the 1960s, his younger colleague Peter has applied his skills to the making of anything from a dinghy to a forty-foot yacht as the business has had to adapt to the demands of the pleasure-craft industry to survive.

**71 Cardiff Boatbuilders Office,
Pictures of Small Craft**

On the wall of the office, these snapshots are reminders of the small fishing/pleasure vessels worked on in more recent times. The business dates back to 1913 when it was founded by Sidney Wright whose design of a life raft after the *Titanic* disaster was adopted by the Admiralty and made standard on British merchant ships. Other achievements over the years include a contract from Canadian Pacific for lifeboats on their passenger liners and the building of two replica lifeboats for the *Cutty Sark* from an 1870s design.

Launch of the *Pembrey*, Cardiff Bay

The last craft to be launched by Cardiff Boat Builders into Cardiff's harbour (or the first to be launched into Cardiff Bay) dangles over the dock wall before being lowered into the water. Originally this was a high-speed RAF motor cruiser used in World War II for rescuing pilots who had ditched into the sea over the English Channel. It is apparently one of six still in existence and was luxuriously restored for the present-day owner of Cardiff Boat Builders.

72 Port Banner, Roath Basin

Roath Basin, opened in 1874, is the only part of the active Port of Cardiff accessible to the general public. Its north quay, renamed Britannia Quay, has been newly landscaped for public use and is a popular visitor attraction with the *Goleulong* lightship moored alongside it. There is no longer any commercial shipping activity to attract the interest of the visitor or maritime enthusiast but visiting vessels such as *HMS Cardiff* and the replica sailing ship *Prince William of Glasgow*, amongst others, pay occasional visits.

Dredger *City of Cardiff*

United Marine Aggregates was the last maritime company to use Roath Basin for stockpiling sand gathered from the floor of the Bristol Channel by vessels such as the *City of Cardiff*. Almost 2 million tons of such sand was used in the building of the Barrage. But behind on the left, the presence of new flats explains why scenes like this have now become a thing of the past. Many more such properties will be built along the quaysides as the demand for a pied à terre by the old docks inexorably increases.

73 Bows of *Goleulong 2000* Lightship

Permanently moored in Roath Basin and one of Cardiff Bay's major attractions, this former lightship was launched in 1953 and last used to protect shipping near the Helwick Sands off Rhossili in the Gower Peninsula. After restoration in the early 1990s, not just as a maritime attraction but also as a Christian Centre, it was towed to Cardiff Bay in 1993 to take on its new role as home to the Churches of Wales. On board facilities include a chapel for quiet prayer as well as a cafeteria. The *Goleulong* ('Lightship' in Welsh) is open to the public free of charge and run by volunteers.

**Lightship Tower and Masts of Sailing Vessel
*Prince William***

The masts of the sailing ship *Prince William* and the beacon tower of *Goleulong 2000* make an interesting combination at their appointed berths in a corner of Roath Basin. Visitors may climb the light tower at any time but climbing the masts of the sailing ship will require rather more special skills and a good head for heights. The *Prince William* trains young people in those kinds of seafaring skills amongst others.

74 Entrance to Roath Dock

Though by no means busy, the working port of Cardiff has consolidated and is diversifying its shipping activity with a certain degree of success. Commodities dealt with in Roath Dock include scrap metal, oil and general cargo. More exciting perhaps is the future prospect of cruise ships calling at Cardiff, with Roath Dock providing the necessary berthing facilitites.

Stern of *Hallgarth* tugboat

The *Hallgarth*, moored here at the west end of Roath Dock near the Missions to Seafarers Centre has been in service for years. Formerly owned by Cory Towage, it was once part of a much larger fleet which all had names ending in 'garth'.

75 *Eversmeer* Loading at Dowlais Wharf

The piles of scrap metal on the north side of Roath Dock are exported to the USA amongst other foreign destinations and there has been an increase in this trade in recent times. These piles of fodder for foreign steelworks actually stand where cranes used to unload iron ore for use in Cardiff's own East Moors Steelworks, closed in 1978. Grabs now work alongside the wharf to load the scrap into the holds of the *Eversmeer*.

Docks Diesel Shunter

The railways, from being an absolutely indispensable means of haulage to and from the docks in the nineteenth and twentieth centuries have now been almost completely replaced by road transport. The flow of lorries through the port check-points is more or less constant. However, there is still a certain amount of freight, mainly steel products, moved by rail on to the sidings and quayside of the Queen Alexandra Dock. But the sight of a vintage Class 08 shunter such as this one is more a reminder of the past than a sign of the future.

76 Demolition of Spillers Mill, Roath Dock, 2002

Known as the 'cathedral of the docks' this imposing landmark, visible for miles from any vantage point in or near Cardiff, had stood at the east end of Roath Dock since 1939. Spillers the grain merchants, makers of sea biscuits, flour, sweet biscuits and dog biscuits had works at various times on three of Cardiff's docks – the East, the West and the Roath. Demolition of this, the last and largest of its grain elevators began in late 2001.

77   **Spillers Mill, 2003**

Demolition is almost complete after many months. Work was delayed for a number of weeks because a protected species of bird was found to be nesting in the tower. When the winged would-be preservationist was gone, demolition resumed.

1905 Pontoon, Roath Dock

A floating dock or pontoon, dating from a century ago and made in Cardiff Docks, spends its last days at Spillers Wharf in Roath Dock.

78   **Channel Dry Dock entrance and St. David's Hotel, Cardiff Bay**

The entrance wall to the old dry dock, clad in wood and cement, contrasts with the Costa-style balconies of St. David's Hotel across Cardiff Bay. Cardiff's five-star hotel is crowned by a large, metallic flight-of-fancy representing a ship's prow cutting through water. Many ships' prows passed through the lock gates of the Channel Dry Dock in the past, some damaged and much in need of the attention of Bristol Channel Ship Repairers, the last owners when it closed in the 1980s.

Barge, Channel Dry Dock

One sign of life around the old dock was still visible in the summer of 2002 and this one quite dramatic. A great metal barge had been lifted onto the edge of the dock before being put up on its side. Barges such as this were used in the construction of the Cardiff Barrage to transport the large stones that form the base of the Barrage approach, which begins not far from the end of the dry dock.

79   **Cardiff Bay Buildings, from Channel Dry Dock**

The wall in the foreground belonged to the ship-repairing bay of the Channel Dry Dock. In the distance the contrast between old and new buildings couldn't be more vivid. The huge modern structure resembling a beached whale glistening in the sun is the Wales Millennium Centre. It is flanked on either side by architectural icons from Cardiff's past – the Pier Head Building (1896) and the Norwegian Church (rebuilt 1989).

Anchors, Lloyds Beal, Dumballs Road

A traditional docklands concern, Lloyds Beal (formerly Beal and Sons) in Dumballs Road is one of the very few still-viable maritime businesses in Cardiff. The yard is piled high with anchor and chain of all weights and sizes, new and second hand for sale to shipping companies. The remarkable sight of these giant, ocean-going relics often attracts the attention of photographers and even the occasional bride and groom who use them as a setting for their wedding photographs.

80   **Quayside, Steel Coils and 'A' Sheds**

The Queen's is the other commercially active dock remaining in the Port of Cardiff. In addition to newer facilities such as its container terminal, older facilities like the landmark transit sheds and quays along the dock's north side continue to play a part in maritime operations. A quantity of steel coil from the resurrected CELSA Steelworks (formerly ASW) awaits shipment.

Oil Tanks, Queen Alexandra Dock

Other structures typical of Cardiff docks are its oil tanks, though some such as these are vintage era and not necessarily in modern-day use. The huge containers and their shadows near the Queen Alexandra Dock make for striking visual compositions.

81   RMS *St. Helena*

Until the end of 2003 the Royal Mail Ship *St. Helena* called at Cardiff three times a year and berthed in the Queen's Dock. She is a supply vessel, part cargo and part passenger ship, providing the only link between the UK and the island of St. Helena in the South Atlantic. She has accommodation for 128 passengers and one-way fares for the two-week cruise to the island started at just under a £1000. During the Falklands War, the St. Helena was requisitioned to serve as a mine-sweeper support vessel. Sailings to/from Cardiff have been temporarily suspended following a trial revision of the ship's timetable, so it remains to be seen whether this exotic visitor will call at Cardiff again.

82   **Lock Supervisor seeing off *Welsh Piper***

The Lock Supervisor is on hand to ensure that the Newport-registered dredger *Welsh Piper* is safely away, having left its berth in Queen Alexandra Dock. It has just cleared the lock gates at the pier head before entering the waters of the Bristol Channel. The dredger will be working in the Channel in one of the areas designated for the removal of sand from its floor. Penarth Head is the familiar landmark in the distance.

Lock Supervisor and Lock Gateman

Posing at the pier head of the Port of Cardiff are the men responsible for the safe entry and departure of ships calling at Cardiff. The photograph, taken in 2002, is of Peter Davis and John Davis (no relation), who have since retired with over 60 years combined service.

Part Three: From Taff to Rhymney: the Edges of Dockland

85   **Swans in the Taff, Clarence Bridge**

Moving from the maritime docks to the residential Docks (the capital 'D' is still used to distinguish between the two) means starting at its western extremity bordered by the River Taff. Like Cardiff's waterfront along its harbour, the banks of the Taff once teemed with maritime-related industry such as the nineteenth-century shipyard of John Batchelor. In the twentieth century large-scale manufacturing took place in the huge Curran works and the John Williams Foundry. But as with the rest of Cardiff's waterfront, this state of affairs has changed dramatically. Hundreds of up-market apartments have replaced old industrial buildings and living with a view over the river is now all the rage. The sight of swans along the Taff, viewed from an apartment balcony or the seat of an excursion boat adds a touch of the bucolic to Cardiff's new maritime-residential chic.

Rear of Bute Esplanade, the Docks

The rear of the Georgian-style terraced houses in Bute Esplanade must now co-exist with the glistening twenty-first-century apartments just a stone's throw away. Their balconies overlook what was once the ship repair yard of Mount Stuart Dry docks. But the traditional residences facing Cardiff's harbour have also seen their values skyrocket as older properties in the midst of new upmarket accommodation have become exceedingly desirable.

86   **Royal Hamadryad Hospital, Rat Island**

The 4th Marquess of Bute proclaimed the hospital open in June, 1902 at a time when Cardiff was approaching its greatest prosperity as the world's largest exporter of coal.

Thousands of seamen would have been working at their hard, often dangerous tasks, subject to disease and injury, and a modern facility dedicated to their well-being was no doubt a welcome amenity. The building replaced the *HMS Hamadryad*, a frigate converted into a hospital ship and hauled up onto the foreshore near the Glamorganshire Canal in the 1860s. When the old ship was removed, so the story goes, the thousands of rats fleeing to land gave the local area its name of Rat Island. The Hamadryad's imperious façade has remained virtually untouched over the many years it has stood in Cardiff's docklands.

Entrance Hall

Unmistakeably from another era, the main hallway into the hospital was still in pristine condition when its doors closed for good in May 2002.

87 Kitchen Staff on the Last Day

On the day of the hospital's closure it was possible to go in to take photographs. The wards and corridors were being emptied by the removal men taking away the furnishings. In the kitchens, however, staff were still there going about their daily tasks.

HMS Hamadryad Plaque

Mounted in the entrance hall for all to see was this delightful plaque, a modern-day commemoration of the good ship *Hamadryad*, resembling a nineteenth-century Noah's Ark, complete with staff and sailors on board. The figurehead of the *Hamadryad* has been preserved and is presently at the National Museum of Wales Collections Centre, Nantgarw, a few miles north of Cardiff.

88 Salvage House, Clarence Road

The last commercial building in Clarence Road before leaving the docks via Clarence Bridge is Salvage House, where the Lloyds Register of Shipping was kept until it was moved to the Collections Centre at Nantgarw. The building shows influences from the Art Deco era and dates from 1922. Behind Salvage House lie the Victorian terraced streets of Rat Island and Clarence Embankment from where this gentleman has just emerged.

Ronnie Keith and Harry Cooke

A familiar figure upon a familiar two-wheeler is Harry Cooke, intermittently stopping to talk to anyone he knows along the way, in this case his Glaswegian friend, Ronnie Keith. Anyone expecting to hear a Cardiff accent, however, is in for a surprise. Not only is Harry an unusual breed in being a well-published and poetic old sea-dog, but he is also a Liverpudlian who has forsaken that once-great English seafaring city for this Welsh one. His commitment to his adopted hometown was put to the test when the bulldozers of the Cardiff Bay Development Corporation arrived to destroy Harry's favourite willow tree at the harbour's edge: he took up his stance in front of the machines and would not budge until they backed off. Although the tree has been felled since, the incident is now a well-known episode in Docks folklore. Plans are afoot to construct a bow-shaped monument to enshrine what remains of the tree, in Harry's honour.

89 Drayman outside 'The White Hart'

Proceeding along James Street takes one past one of the Docks last remaining pubs, 'The White Hart'. Here the drayman standing by his vehicle from the local Brains brewery takes a breather after lowering barrels of beer into the cellar of 'The White Hart'.

Sixth Formers at 'The Ship and Pilot'

I include myself in the large number of locals who have encountered school groups from the foreign confines of England come to do a survey about the new Cardiff Bay. One of the inevitable questions is: Do you think that the amount of money spent on Cardiff Bay is justified? Standing outside 'The Ship and Pilot', one of the very last Docks pubs left to serve local residents when so many others have been sacrificed to development schemes which are clearly not for the benefit of local Docks people, there can only be one answer. 'The Ship and Pilot' closed in its turn in late 2004.

90 Former Canal Warehouses near James Street

The Royal Stuart Warehouses (1899) once graced the borders of the Glamorganshire Canal as it followed its course through Butetown towards the Sea Lock and Cardiff's harbour. At nearby James Street, to this day a busy thoroughfare, there was once a swing bridge allowing canal and road traffic to coexist in this part of the Docks.

Tourist Bus and former Pumping Station

Dating from the nineteenth century and once the pumping station for the Mount Stuart Dry Docks, the disused building was reborn as the Sports Café in the 1990s, a high-profile café/bar that seems to have set the precedent for a number of other similar watering holes on the Cardiff waterfront. The Sports Café even provided sponsorship for Cardiff City Football Club for a season or two. For whatever reason, it didn't last. Nonetheless, it lies on the itinerary of the Cardiff Sightseeing Tour where the real object of interest at this point is probably the new block of superflats in front of the tour bus and the five-star St. David's Hotel it has just left behind.

91 St. Stephen's Hall and Church signboard

The last piece of evidence for a once-thriving Docks place of worship. St. Stephen's Hall is just behind the Royal Stuart Warehouses whilst the former church is in Mount Stuart Square. St. Stephen's has been converted to a performance venue known as 'The Point'.

92 Post Office Pillars, Bute Place

The pillars will be known by older residents as belonging to the old Butetown post office, closed in the 1980s. Replaced since then by a minuscule facility just around the corner in Bute Street this grandiose building also had a more exalted function. It was originally built in 1874 as the Mercantile Marine Building, where the signing on/off of sailors going to and coming from sea took place. In contrast with the classical lines of its colonnade through which dockers and seafarers once passed, the massive contours of the Millennium Centre take shape as it becomes the dominant presence on the Docklands skyline.

Rear of Louisa Place Estate, James Street

The long, rather inhospitable-looking brick facade at the rear of Louisa Place on the south side of James Street dates from the late 1970s. It replaced the old James Street shops and businesses which had fallen on hard times, superseding the grid of terraced streets, including Louisa Street, running at right angles off James Street.

93 Post Office detail

Though relentlessly deteriorating, the fabric of the building still has this and other embellishments that speak of the craftsmanship and attention to detail typical of its era.

Railings in Bute Crescent

Unchanged from when I first photographed them in the 1970s and dating from many decades before then, they remain in place in Bute Crescent even though the street itself has seen many changes.

94   Cycle Route Signpost, Lloyd George Avenue

A hundred yards or so north of the Oval Basin, where ships once entered the Bute West Dock, one is confronted by the stunningly blank façades of Atlantic Wharf Leisure Complex. Here, in an American Mall-type setting, leisure-seekers, drinkers and diners will find a 24-lane bowling alley, a multi-screen cinema, bars and restaurants. Outside, along the path of the Taff Trail/National Cycle Route, stands this signpost to guide the cyclist, a brave David on two wheels threatened by the Goliath of new roads and incessant four-wheeled traffic that now overrun this part of the Docklands.

Cardiff Bay (former Bute Road) Station Canopy, New Apartments

The wooden canopy belongs to the former Bute Road Station (now Cardiff Bay Station) and shelters the long-disused though still-existent platforms. Who knows what its future will be. Meanwhile, in the background, the apartments that stretch the length of the recently-built Lloyd George Avenue have gone up seemingly without a hitch and new owners have moved in to their fashionable Docklands flats.

95   Pier Head Building, National Assembly Debating Chamber Site

Construction work, as indicated by the crane gantry, has begun on the National Assembly Debating Chamber, touted as a twenty-first-century 'masterpiece' and scheduled to open in 2005 adjacent to the 1896-vintage Pier Head Building. It will be intriguing to see whether the styles of the two will somehow complement each other. Will the Pier Head Building maintain any sort of prominence in the midst of the large-scale, late-model edifices that are its nearest neighbours?

New Construction in Lloyd George Avenue

As the last of the new apartments takes shape, their position and the view that new occupants will enjoy of the nearby landmark towers of St. Mary's in Bute Street becomes apparent. The Church will no doubt be happy to minister to the spiritual needs of those new Docklands residents wishing to make the short journey across Lloyd George Avenue and over to Bute Street to attend services.

96   Football Coaches, Lloyd George Avenue

The present day spectacle of coaches parked nose to tail along the new Lloyd George Avenue, near the site of the former West Dock, invites comparison with the sailing vessels that tied up at its wharves in much the same way 150 years ago. Near the same location as these coaches, ships returning to Cardiff from Ireland in the mid-nineteenth century were loaded with human ballast – Irish families escaping the Potato Famine and labourers imported by the Marquis of Bute to help with the building of his docks. Now in the twenty-first century, the human ballast of these diesel-powered, modern day transporters of people is made up of football or rugby fans bound for the Millennium Stadium.

Redundant Road Signs, Butetown

Collingdon Road, a rough, gritty, stretch of tarmac once running parallel to the Bute West Dock and serving its quays, factories and warehouses, is now 'closed' because it has been expensively reincarnated as the four-lane Lloyd George Avenue. 'Reuniting the City with its Waterfront' is the catchphrase supposedly relevant to its function. Letton Road was named after a local character, Tommy Letton, who used to sell fish from his barrow in the streets of Tiger Bay. His road now begins on the other side of Lloyd George Avenue, outside of his native Butetown.

97   Father and Son, English Football Fans

Having just got off the coach and heading for the Millennium Stadium, this happy duo are no doubt oblivious to the history of the ground on which they walk. Behind them, Lloyd George Avenue is adorned every hundred yards or so by relics such as anchors and clamshell buckets, presumably from scrapped dockside cranes. Visitors such as these will perhaps occupy a small place in history themselves as part of a phenomenon not seen before the twenty-first century in Cardiff – hoards of English football fans coming to Wales to see their teams play in finals while waiting for a new Wembley Stadium to be built. Ten years ago, who would have imagined this scene in the Docks?

Passage between Lloyd George Avenue and Bute Street

The passage is seen here before its eventual refurbishment. It provides a pedestrian/cycle link between Lloyd George Avenue and Bute Street, passing under the railway embankment that carries trains to Cardiff Bay Station. A young lad on his bicycle is using the old passage to his advantage as he approaches the Bute Street estate (former Tiger Bay) seen in the background.

98   Sacks of Potatoes, Edward England Warehouse Interior

Inside the storage area a few months before closure.

99   Edward England Warehouse Exterior

Named after its founder Edward who started the business in 1842 and then Major England who took over the business in 1935, this is one of two stone warehouses on the former West Dock to survive into the twenty-first century. The rounded, dressed-stone corners of the structure give it its distinctive appearance. In its heyday, over 30 ships a month brought Irish potatoes to the England Wharf. Intended for miners in the Valleys as well Cardiff's markets, they were shovelled from their holds by Irish women, living just a few yards away in the Newtown community. The building was still in use by Edward England Ltd in 2002 after 160 years but then sold for conversion into yet more luxury flats. After the building was sold and Cardiff City Council was informed of the plans to convert it, one Councillor, born in the Docks, was reported to have stated his desire for part of the building to be made into a city museum. Now there's an idea.

Interior Detail

By now a museum piece, a sign that will hopefully not be discarded when conversion takes place.

100   Herbert Street and Tyndall Street, former Newtown

This was the southern boundary of the former Newtown, or 'Little Ireland', when it was a working-class community of just six streets only a hundred yards from the West Dock. Although there is hardly a trace left, the terraced houses having been bulldozed in the 1960s, former residents still keep in contact via the Newtown Association. After it was cleared the area was used as gypsy caravan site in the 1970s but then was eventually transformed into the Tyndall Street Industrial Estate of today, some units of which are in the background. A new bus stop straddles the meeting point of the two old streets.

Employees, Tyndall Street Industrial Estate

Clad in the hygienic protective wear their job requires, this pair of young ladies are on their break at the Nature's Table health food processing plant. It is one of many small businesses in the purpose-built industrial units on the site. Light industry and commerce no longer requires the muscle-power of the heavy industrial and maritime workforce of yesteryear.

101 ### Ladies on steps of the Newtown Footbridge

When I photographed here in the 1970s, I came across two gypsy girls who were playing house at the bottom of these steps, their game disturbed only by the very occasional pedestrian. Now the footbridge is a busy link between the new offices and businesses of Tyndall Street Industrial Estate and the city centre. Frequent human traffic must also have been the case over a century ago when the footbridge was first built over the main London to South Wales railway line. Historically speaking, the ladies are walking up from what was once Pendoylan Place on Newtown's northern edge.

Demolition Team and Passing Ladies, Herbert Street

This was not just an isolated occasion. With so many older properties being demolished, new ones being constructed and sites being worked on right from the centre of Cardiff down to its waterfront, it was and still is typical for people going about their everyday business to encounter the incessant noise, dust and proximity of men and machines at work. It appears that these ladies are getting as much attention as they could want.

102 ### Demolished Timber Merchant's Offices, Herbert Street

Opposite the Edward England warehouse and next to the Herbert Street bridge over the docks feeder, these were the remains in 2002 of a timber merchant's offices. At one time this was an important Cardiff industry, processing timber kept in the nearby ponds of the Glamorganshire Canal. The site is now familiar to people working locally and to shoppers as a car park.

103 ### Power Station, East Tyndall Street Bridge

From an elevated vantage point where Tyndall Street Crossing used to be, the view towards the city brings the eye into contact with a power station consciously designed as a work of art. One of the first if not the first of Cardiff's public art works commissioned under the auspices of CBAT (Cardiff Bay Arts Trust) this is 'Blue Flash' by John Gingell. The poster in the foreground indicates the modern-day raison d'être of one of the Docks' seminal institutions, the Coal Exchange. Local graffiti adds another dimension. At ground level on the other side of the bridge was a small industrial backwater containing a few remains of what industrial and maritime Cardiff was once all about. I thought I had seen the last of this area's working origins clustered around the East Dock, its railways and wagons, the steelworks, industrial workshops, scrapyards, workers' cafés and pubs, warehouses. Though the vast majority of these were defunct or gone by the year 2000, a few, surprisingly, remained.

Demolition worker

Demolition crews have been wreaking destruction and wielding power akin to the Almighty in Cardiff for the past two decades – at the behest of developers.

104 ### Jaki and Rosemary, East Dock/Mossi's café

The corrugated metal, portakabin-style eatery dated from the early 1980s when the business belonged to Rosemary's

father Modestino Cucciniello. Having immigrated from Italy to Britain in the early 1950s, he first bought the café from two sisters in 1964 and it was thereafter known as 'Mossi's'. When the first café burnt to the ground, it was replaced by the structure in the photograph. The rudimentary shutters folded down, and there was never anything less than a smile from the two ladies on hand when the first blue-collar customers arrived at 8.30am

Rosemary and Marina

Rosemary and Marina with two of perhaps 50 that were served daily. Tools and equipment for a six-hour non-stop shift: larder fridge and freezer, two cookers, no microwave. Two huge frying pans for the sausage, bacon, black pudding, fried bread, mushrooms and eggs, two deep saucepans for the stewed tomatoes and beans, two deep-fat fryers for the chips, an industrial size toaster for the never-ending rounds.

105 ### Breakfast at Mossi's café

Big bottles of sauce, lots of white bread and butter, always plenty on your plate, never anything left over. Seven bench-style tables with formica tops, warped, dark veneer wallboard and part of the ceiling hanging down at the back, pegboard menus, portable gas fire for the winter, ventilation when the door was open, a leaking roof on rainy days, but warmth, a feeling of being well-fed and well-looked after. For a cup of tea: go to the counter, ask for a mug of tea. Jaki or Rose or Marina pours boiling hot water into a mug, drops in a teabag and puts it in front of you with a 'there we are, a'right' love, help yourself to milk and sugar'. When tea bag has mashed long enough, take it out, squeeze and leave it in a small bowl on the counter. Add milk (from a 4 pint plastic bottle) and sugar (from a gallon-sized bowl) to taste. Stir and return teaspoon to sugar bowl. If you want coffee do it yourself from the kettle and catering size jar on the counter. Sit down, have a chat, a joke, a moan, a smoke, read the *Sun*, drink your tea/coffee as you wait for breakfast. Won't be long.

Harry, Tugboat Crewman

'Harry? He's about seventy but if he's away for very long it means he's gone back to work on the tugboats,' says Jaki. He knew Mossi, Rosemary's father, back in the days he had the café. He tells the story of a regular customer who, on a very cold day, took off his coat and draped it over the burning portable gas fire. When a startled Mossi asked him what he was doing he replied: 'That poor little fire. It's so bloody cold I'm trying to keep it warm!'

106 ### Talking about Mossi's

Towards the end of the working day and the café almost empty, a local lady becomes indignant over its impending demise. The subject of conversation was Mossi's versus McDonald's, the alternative venue for breakfast once Mossi's has gone unless it's the burger vans. According to this lady one big advantage of Mossi's was the open-plan kitchen, where you can see exactly what's going on, as well as the conversation, home-cooked food, etc. As for me, I was able to go and photograph anywhere I wanted in that café.

Last Day, Empty Tables

'Where do we go when Rose has gone?' Typical question heard from regulars at these tables in the weeks before the last day. Rosemary and Jaki have packed away moveable items cutlery, crockery, and taken the menus as keepsakes before leaving never to return. Rosemary can't afford to start up again elsewhere. Compulsory purchase of the site didn't include compensation for the loss of her business.

Jaki will rely on working in the local supermarket to support her family.

107 Dale, Motor Engineer, Pogson's Engineering

Although only in his late twenties, Dale's situation harks back to former times when young men wanting to learn a highly-skilled job did so in the place of work, instructed by their elders and serving an apprenticeship. Nowadays young men wanting to do the same would need to go on a training course, do work experience and gain a diploma before going out in search of work.

108 Lou Pogson

Son of the original founder of the business, Lou exercised his skills in the old workshop for over 30 years before it was forced to close down in mid-2003 and then relocated outside Cardiff. His skills, which here involve calibrating a crankshaft, will have disappeared from the Docklands with him. The door to this 1940s-era engineering works was just a few yards from Mossi's Café. The two businesses side by side were a fascinating but not untypical pair of docklands survivors. They were demolished within days of each other.

Piston-boring Machine

About as high-tech as you'll get in Pogson's. Much of the machinery was still original from the post-war years.

109 Hand Tools, Pogson's Workshop

Aesthetics and functionality come together on Pogson's workshop wall.

Pogson's Demolished Works, East Docks Café

Machines and skilled human activity gone from this place forever, Pogson's took a couple of days to demolish. Mossi's café took a couple of hours. A car dealership now holds sway.

110 Derek and Louise Davies, Machinery Movements Crane Hire

The last of the small, family-run East Dock businesses forced to relocate or die was Machinery Movements, founded in 1982 by the present proprietor Derek Davies. In a brick cabin where railway workers once clocked on and off, the company office was installed. If behind every good man there is a good woman, in this case it's the boss's daughter Louise, who handles much of the day-to-day running of her father Derek's business. Being an attractive young female working in a less-than-glamorous world of men handling 40-ton cranes doesn't bother her in the least. In fact she rather enjoys running the show.

Crane Driver

The yard in which these cranes are parked was (for at least a century) railway land covered by sidings leading to the steelworks and docks. By the end of the 1970s most of these had gone, leaving space available for the crane-hire business to establish itself. Here crane driver John Ford threads heavy wire rope through a pully block as he changes the hook on his machine to a bigger one.

111 Crane Yard worker

Machinery Movements managed to find a new plot near Roath Dock from which to continue operating. It's moving day and the worker is waiting to secure hooks to the side of a container before it can be raised on to a flatbed lorry.

John Sennett, Adamsdown Historian, 'The Great Eastern' pub

Made redundant in 2002 from the Tremorfa steelworks where he was a locomotive driver, John now devotes a great deal of time to his hobby – researching the history of Adamsdown. He has compiled and carefully catalogued an enormous amount of material on the area tracing it back to its medieval origins. Sitting with a pint at 'The Great Eastern', his local and the oldest surviving building in Adamsdown, John displays pages from one of his compilations. His work continues, whereas the pub has now finished trading.

112 Young Mum and Friend on the Black Bridge, Adamsdown

When this footbridge carried the heavy-duty workforce of Adamsdown to the steelworks, docks and railways (a scenario still vivid in the memory of older local residents) this scene of young motherhood would have been highly unexpected. But with these industries having declined drastically or disappeared, its pedestrian traffic has taken on a different character. New housing built in the last ten years on both sides of the bridge means that Emma and Rebecca with babies in pushchairs are the more typical users of today. They were scarcely aware that East Moors steelworks had ever existed. Since this photo was taken, the bleak look of the corrugated siding has been replaced by barriers of much more attractive design and decorated by young artists from the East Moors Community Centre.

113 Young Muslim on the Black Bridge

Another image hinting at recent changes in the social makeup of Adamsdown. The community is now more racially-mixed than it was a quarter of a century ago, as is typical of most of the city's communities.

Gospel Hall, Kames Place

One of the most familiar Adamsdown landmarks, the Gospel Hall, opened in 1877, is still serving its religious community. When the Black Bridge was built in the early 1890s and immediately used daily by hoards of workmen, the path to it was at the rear of the hall. The main entrance was therefore changed around so that it faced the path, enabling the gospel brethren to distribute leaflets and speak to the men as they passed by. A shrewd move which lead to a significant increase in the congregation.

114 Yvonne Camilleri, Adamsdown Resident

The lady in curlers holding a cup of tea in the 1970s photograph decided not to adopt the same attire in 2002. What comes across this time is the dignity and bearing of the undisputed matriarch – a source of serenity, affection and gentle humour for all those around her.

115 Camilleri Family and Friends, Garesfield Street

As they were the family on the cover of *Before the Deluge* it was particularly pleasing to find that Camilleris of the younger generation still occupied the same house and could be photographed in the same location. In fact most of the family and friends in the 1970s photograph continue to live near each other in Adamsdown. Janine and Tony Camilleri, on the left, organized a gathering together of the original group as well as wives, husbands, partners and children so that a modern-day version of the 1970s photo could be taken. That meant photographing 25 bodies and faces of all ages instead of seven. A daunting task for the photographer but with gratifying results, showing a large Cardiff family in its glory.

Adamsdown children, Anderson Field

There are organizations and initiatives within the community that provide services to its young people and promote constructive, high-profile community projects. One of these was Adamsdown Arts Week 2002 during which pupils, some of whom are pictured here, painted a superb mural on the walls of the new Anderson Place housing estate. Adamsdown has set an example, it seems, for other such initiatives in the city.

116   Detail in South Luton Place

Over the doorways along the traditional street, the neo-classical scrollwork adds an aristocratic touch to the Victorian working-class frontages. It was once typical to add small-scale distinguishing characteristics such as these to each street of terraced houses.

Sikh Gentleman in South Luton Place

A member of Cardiff's Sikh community. For him as for other local residents the pavement is, in fine weather, virtually an extension of the front sitting room.

117   Loan Shop, Constellation Street, Adamsdown

Pertuce Loan Company is on the end of Constellation Street, the last building in the terrace all built of the same stone. This is one of several named after elements of the heavens – System, Sun, Eclipse being others. Moon and Cycle streets are now of the past.

Moira Hotel, Moira Terrace

An Adamsdown landmark, local historian John Sennett tells me it was occupied by 1861, closed in 1999 and demolished in 2002. The name Moira probably derives from the Earl of Moira who had connections with the Bute family. The hotel has given way, like so many older buildings and sites in south Cardiff, to the construction of new flats.

118   Loretta and Dorothy Chambers, Splott

Two sisters, former residents of Lower Splott, forced to move with their families in the 1970s when compulsory purchase orders led to the demolition of their homes, stand at the park gates which mark almost exactly the location of Loretta's former house on the corner of Neath and Milford streets. I photographed her there in 1975 with members of her family, not realizing that demolition was imminent. The extended family which Loretta and Dorothy belonged to once occupied five different houses in Aberystwith Street.

Chambers Sisters, Pointing at their Initials

As we walked through a deserted Moorland Park where the animated streets of their old neighbourhood once provided the community's fabric, Loretta, Dorothy and I came to a wooden telephone pole where the two sisters rediscovered the initials they had carved in it as young girls some 45 years ago.

119   Graham Kingston of Aberystwith Street

Certain streets in the Welsh capital have curious anglicized spellings, Redlaver (Rhydlafar) in Grangetown being another example. This particular street in Lower Splott is one of only two, with Aberdovey Street, that have survived intact after this part of Cardiff was almost totally demolished in the 1970s. Destruction did in fact affect this end of the street when it was bombed during World War II. As seen here, some of its houses were rebuilt in brick: a contrast with the nineteenth-century stone-built houses across the street that suffered no damage. Aberystwith Street and its older residents such as Graham Kingston have seen many changes, notably the closing of nearby East Moors steelworks in 1978 which drastically affected the future of the community. The steelworks was only a few hundred yards away from this end of Aberystwith Street.

Playing in Aberystwith Street

With little traffic in the street now that it is a cul-de-sac, and with the old paving stones replaced by smooth tarmac, playing on your new micro-scooter is popular and relatively safe. Letting the dog out is relatively safe too. The tranquility of this scene speaks of a way of life far removed from the days when the din, pollution and looming forms of East Moors Steelworks against the sky in the background dominated everyday activity. The streets were often covered in red dust.

120   Ken Norton, Heavyweight Boxer at 'The New Fleurs' Club, Splott

'The New Fleurs' Club, one of two surviving local amenities in Lower Splott, is very much at the heart of its social life. But apart from being a place where locals drink and socialize, it also plays host to more uncommon events such as the visit of the boxer Ken Norton, who once defeated Muhammed Ali. The contacts in the boxing world which the club's recently retired owner Dai Furnish enjoyed brought Ken and his manager to the club during a UK tour of boxing exhibitions by the former heavyweight. During the course of the evening he happily chatted with the locals and signed autographs, including this pair of boxing gloves for the Welsh Ex-Boxers Association.

Rita, formerly of Newtown, at 'The New Fleurs'

Rita Perry is a resident of the CCHA's Selwyn Morris Court, just across Portmanmoor Road from the Fleurs. An ex-Newtown girl, she was born in Herbert Street in a boarding house for ships' crew, dockers and stokers. Brought up in Pendoylan Place she was one of the last to leave the minuscule Irish community when it was demolished in the 1960s. Her liveliness and humorous imparting of stories about her old neighbourhood are a delight to experience. Her favorite recollection is of her grandmother, an elegant woman whose sense of pride and decency was severely tested when she had to pawn her husband's waistcoat to put food on the table. When she got it back from the pawnbroker's there was a gold sovereign in the pocket which grandpa had put there for safekeeping. Rita does volunteer work at the Heath Hospital where she is a League of Friends Welcomer. She is also Secretary of the Tenants' Association of Selwyn Morris Court.

121   Beryl and her Tattoos, 'The New Fleurs' Club

There is a large function room upstairs in 'The Fleurs' and any event there brings local people together in numbers that are perhaps not possible anywhere else in this particular community. Allowed to photograph at a 60th birthday function I met Beryl who, at the age of 74, decided that she would like to have a tattoo – or two. She is reputed to be the most senior lady in Cardiff to have done this and is obviously proud of the fact. Beryl is also a resident of Selwyn Morris Court.

122   Statue and Caravan, Rover Way Gypsy Site

Cardiff has two of the UK's sixteen caravan sites for its Welsh Gypsies. This one in Rover Way, at the eastern extremity of Splott, is just a hammer-throw from Cardiff's heavy metal industry – Sims Metal Recycling and Tremorfa Steelworks. In existence since the 1980s, the purpose-built amenity replaced the Tyndall Street camp sprawled on the derelict land left by the demolition of Newtown. Now the caravans park on a concrete surface and are provided with electricity, running water and sanitary facilities. In addition to the pristine caravans that make up family accommodation, an eye-catching touch of individuality and garden kitsch has been added to this one in the shape of ornamental statues.

Daily Cleaning, Rover Way
One of the regular daily chores is the ritual scrubbing of the front steps as well as the pressure washing of the caravans, vehicles and hard surface around them. Pride is obviously taken in the spotless appearance of the home and its immediate surroundings.

123 **Tom Price and two Grandsons**
The grand old man of the Rover Way site, Tom Price sometimes uses a large black pot over an open fire right at the entrance to the Rover Way site to cook his stew. Once on the boil, it will bubble away for hours in full view of the passing traffic and this caught my eye one cold February morning as I drove past. After a couple of visits to the site and at Tom's bidding, two of the youngsters (Creggy on the left, Hendry on the right) had their photo taken with their grandfather. The older of the two (Hendry) was fascinated by the photographs I had taken of the Tyndall Street site in the 1970s even though this was well before his time.

Tom Price and his Gypsy Stallion
Across Rover Way is open land on which horses and goats graze. Tom, who was once a horse dealer, looks after them and goes every day to see that they haven't come to any harm, often covering a good deal of ground on foot given the sizeable acreage of the area. At certain times he keeps one or two animals in a homemade corral. The long mane, shaggy feet, and small but stocky size are typical of a gypsy stallion.

124 **Baby Agnes and her Grandad**
She is the newest arrival in the gypsy family and a handful, or rather armful, for her grandad.

Trisha Smith and Children
The dark, Romany attributes of Trisha Smith and her children are evident. So is her good humour and willingness to pose for the camera. She is pictured here with her two young sons Henry (second left) and Dino (first right) and two of their young cousins.

125 **Trisha Smith**
A portrait reveals her striking features. Trisha says that she is from a long line of Romany descent and that her parents were travellers throughout Britain before she eventually settled down at the Rover Way site. She is resigned to the fact that the itinerant lifestyle involved in 'travelling' is a thing of the past and now part of gypsy folklore.

Agnes Coffey with her Daughter, Helen
Having known the Tyndall Street site in the 1970s Agnes Coffey was interested in my photographs taken there in 1974. Passing family history on to your children is an important priority for Gypsy parents and Helen is a willing listener.

126 **Small Craft on the River Rhymney**
Emptying into the Bristol Channel near the Rover Way site, the Rhymney remains the only one of Cardiff's three rivers to be affected by the tide now that the rise and fall of the two others, the Taff and Ely, have been negated by the Barrage. Small craft such as this still have unhindered access to the Bristol Channel and are often to be seen resting on the estuarial mud of the Rhymney's river flats at low tide, reminiscent of similar scenes from the past in Cardiff's Inner Harbour.

Foreshore near Rover Way
The wish to view the rise and fall of the tide along Cardiff's foreshore in an undisrupted habitat means finding vantage points east of the Barrage. Not the easiest thing to do given that there are no beaches or public access and most of the shoreline is taken up by either the docks or the remains of Cardiff's heavy industry. Nonetheless, beyond the bleak setting of the Tremorfa Industrial Estate and viewed from Cardiff's old landfill site, the ebb and flow of the Channel's waters continues undisturbed, the sun glowing on the smooth alluvial mud, its surface etched by intricate rivulets. In an unexpected and isolated place, a serene and peaceful sight seemingly impervious to the passage of time and man-made changes.

ALSO FROM SEREN

Real Cardiff Peter Finch

Peter Finch discovers the real Cardiff – lost rivers,
Roman forts, holy wells, itinerant poets, the redeveloped Cardiff Bay – as he travels the city from east to
west and north to south. This is offbeat topographical
writing, guaranteed to enthrall the native, the visitor
and the armchair traveller. It's celebratory, it's
subversive, it's Real Cardiff.
"… a marvellous book – one of the very best books
about a city I have ever read." – Jan Morris.

Real Cardiff Two Peter Finch

In further explorations, Finch traverses the capital,
visiting the parts the tourist guides don't tell you about,
mapping a fast-changing city, looking to the future while
remembering how things used to be. He plots the
ancient town walls, takes in the view from the roof of
the new Wales Millennium Centre, meets Billy the Seal
in the National Museum, and investigates the ancient
cairn at Tinkinswood. Irreverent, insightful, and end-
lessly revealing.

A Whim Set in Concrete Sian Best

Was the £200 million plus spent on the Cardiff Bay
Barrage value for money? Not to mention the £21
million annual running bill. And the cost was not just
financial. Irreplaceable wildlife habitats have been
destroyed. Parts of the city faces increased risk from
rising groundwater. Democracy itself has suffered. Sian
Best threads her way through the maze of arguments,
procedures and political machinations and asks essential
questions about the management of the barrage scheme,
the expense and the effect on the people of Cardiff. This
is an eye-opening account of what happens when 'ordi-
nary people' oppose the wishes of an unregulated
developer, and a fascinating insight into the issues and
mechanisms of politics.

The Big Book of Cardiff
Edited by Peter Finch

Published June 2005 – a bumper anthology featuring the
best poets and novelists the city has produced in the
post-war era. Guilt, passion, love, despair, humour,
anger and not a little tenderness from the writers who
put Cardiff on the literary map.